Herbs
& Spices

Herbs & Spices

*How to make the
best use of
herbs and spices in
your cooking*

Christian Teubner
Countess Dr. Sybil Schönfeldt
Dr. Ulrich Gerhardt and Daniel Rühlemann

With recipes by Eckart Witzigmann

PENGUIN
STUDIO

PENGUIN STUDIO
Published by the Penguin Group
Penguin Books USA Inc., 375 Hudson Street,
New York, New York, 10014, U.S.A.

Penguin Books Ltd, 27 Wrights Lane,
London W8 5TZ, England

Penguin Books Australia Ltd,
Ringwood, Victoria, Australia

Penguin Books Canada Ltd,
2801 John Street, Markham, Ontario,
Canada L3R 1B4

Penguin Books (N.Z.) Ltd,
182-90 Wairau Road, Auckland 10, New Zealand

Penguin Books Ltd, Registered Offices:
Harmondsworth, Middlesex, England

First published by Penguin Studio, an imprint of
Penguin Books USA Inc.

First printing, January 1997
10 9 8 7 6 5 4 3 2 1

Original edition published under title
"Kräuter und Knoblauch"
© 1993 Teubner Edition, Germany

English language text
© 1996 Transedition Ltd., England
All rights reserved

Library of Congress Catalog Card Number: 96–67513

ISBN 0-670-87105-2

Printed in Italy

This book is a reference book and cookbook for
culinary herbs. It is not a medical handbook.
The authors, publishers and booksellers cannot
be held responsible for the use of any herbs
mentioned in this book in any manner other
than that given in the recipes.

CONTENTS

The importance that was attached to herbs in the Middle Ages is demonstrated in various books on herbs that were produced at that time, with considerable effort, such as the Eicones Plantarum *by* Tabernaemontanus, *illustrated here, which dates from 1590.*

THE HISTORY OF HERBS

The history of herbs begins in Paradise, in the land between the Euphrates and Tigris rivers, where many people believe the Garden of Eden was located. Some eleven thousand years before Christ, people lived there and cultivated foodstuffs. However, the climate was not settled and the rainfall, irrigation from rivers, and the walls that were built to shelter the gardens from the eroding effect of the wind did not always suffice to protect the harvest. Prayers to the god of the city for greater protection for the gardens of vegetables and herbs were engraved on stone tablets, and the scent of herbs, which was supposed to delight the gods, is mentioned on scroll seals. This shows the importance that was attached to herbs since the beginning of recorded history. Everything that was known about them was noted and handed down from one generation to the next, in these and neighboring lands.

In ancient Sumer herbs were used for

medicinal purposes, and, later, in Babylon herbs and spices were so valued that at the time of Hammurabi men boasted of owning their own houses where such provisions grew so rampantly "that it is like the Tigris in flood." The herbs in question may well have been those listed as growing in the garden of Merodachbaladan in Assyria: garlic, onions and leeks, dill, cardamom, saffron, thyme, and caraway.

Herbs and knowledge of them continued to develop over the centuries. They were brought westwards by the caravans wandering over the various trade routes to Egypt, where garlic was extremely popular, and peppermint and celery were so prized that they were buried, in dried form, with the pharaohs. From Egypt they spread, probably by courtesy of the seafaring Phoenicians, to Greece. In that most civilized land the laurel became the plant associated with Dionysus and Apollo; victors in sport and battle were awarded laurel wreaths; the best cuts of meat were grilled on the embers of laurel branches; and when a young man visited his beloved, he chewed bay (a variety of laurel) leaves so his breath would smell "heavenly".

Just as important as the religious, social, and domestic functions of herbs was the fact that the ancient Greeks continued to use them for medicinal purposes. Hippocrates, the most notable physician of the ancient world and generally regarded as the father of modern medicine, together with his pupils, founded a medical school in the fifth century BC that was famed far and wide. In many of the various works ascribed to him he brought together all that was then known about herbs, and described their use for the maintenance and restoration of health. His theory of the four humors and their qualities became the basis for Western medicine. Even if we no longer believe that good health is determined by the balance of the four elements — cold and warmth, dryness and dampness — in our bodily fluids, we still use many of the herbs he recommended.

A century after Hippocrates, Theophrastus, the father of ancient botany, reported on the growing of herbs in the Greek garden cities and in Asia Minor in his book *Historia Plantarum*. In the first century AD there were several works that listed and described as many as six hundred herbs. Dioskorides, author of *De Materia Medica*, also gave advice on growing and harvesting herbs, and storing them.

The knowledge of how to use herbs in cooking to enhance and refine the flavor of foods was developed by the Greeks and acquired from them by the Romans. One work, which has become known as the first cookery book, written by one Marcus Apicius, introduced order to cookery. In this book and others, authors encapsulated in recipes the wealth, refined feasting, and exhibitionism of the caesars. When the Romans moved their armies of conquest north, their cooks brought with them not only their knowledge of recipes and their supplies of herbs, dried or preserved in salt or oil, but also the living plants, which they cultivated in the lands they occupied. Thus new herbs spread throughout Europe.

IN THE MONASTERY GARDEN

After the fall of the Roman Empire in the fifth century AD, when the Goths plundered Rome, people emigrated across every border, and the intellectual wealth of the ancient world might eventually have been lost if it were not for St Benedict and his monastery at Monte Cassino. There, from the early sixth century onwards, the monks recorded current learning and preserved the knowledge of the past, copying out works by Ovid and Horace as well as the twelve books of Junius Moderatus Columella from Cadiz, who lived in Syria for many years and who brought together everything that was known in his day about agriculture and gardening. Thus the Benedictines became the inheritors and guardians of antiquity, and the teachers of Europe in the early Middle Ages. They founded monasteries in Gaul and Germania, and had most contact with the Franks.

Charlemagne made use of the monks' great store of knowledge, and the *Decree on Estates* is the result of this collaboration. In this document Charlemagne, who wanted to unite his great empire, and, indeed, compel it to remain united, specified down to the smallest detail what should be planted in fields, villages and monastery gardens, what should be eaten, and what should be set aside as stores. Tenants on the Emperor's estates had to plant specific herbs, vegetables, flowers, trees, and shrubs. Included in the list of herbs were clover and lady's mint, lilies and roses, sage and knotgrass, star anise and black caraway, rosemary and cress, arugula and fennel, endive and peppermint, parsley, myrrh, sandalwood and mustard, hedgerow ferns and yarrow, marshmallow, leek, garlic and chervil, coriander, shallots and sleeping poppy. It was a regular Garden of Eden, which came supplied with a layout. The plan was well-suited to the monastery, comprising a rectangle intersected by two paths. At the center a spring bubbled, a fountain played, or a circular bed blossomed

Most of the prescribed plant species were completely new to the Franks. They came to know them first by their Latin names, but just as their own language had been altered and

A hand-colored illustration of basil from the first German edition of the herbal of Andrea Matholi.

The fact that herbs such as dill were cultivated in Italy in the Middle Ages is shown in this illustration from the housekeeping book of the Cerruti family, from the fourteenth century (Austrian National Library, Vienna).

enriched by the migration of people, they adopted the plants and herbs into their own culture by giving them new descriptive names. This process was to be repeated in many lands over time, which accounts for the great number of different common names by which individual plants are known throughout the world.

A PLAN THAT PREVAILED FOR A THOUSAND YEARS

The text of the estates decree was copied out more and more, and spread from monastery to monastery. Shortly after the death of Charlemagne the decree was used as the basis of the layout for a rich Benedictine monastery at St. Gallen, Switzerland. In the St. Gallen plan, which was not in fact realized in St. Gallen itself but in the fertile climate of nearby Reichenau Island, the kitchen garden was separated from the garden for medicinal herbs for the first time. This was because the care of the sick had now become the responsibility of

the monasteries, which also lead to an initial contrast between the scientists, such as St. Hildegard of Bingen, and the "wise women" or "old wives".

"OLD WIVES'" TALES

It is estimated that in the Middle Ages about only 1 percent of the population in Europe belonged to the nobility or to a religious order, while up to 80 percent of the population were peasant farmers, who grew the crops and tended the animals that provided food for the nobility as well as for themselves. Children and elderly people were often excused from heavy work in the fields, but instead were obliged to gather wild fruits, berries, and leaves — whatever was in season — from the woods and meadows. The season began with the first warm days, when the young stinging nettles or the first young sorrel and salad leaves pushed through the ground. Even the rules of St. Benedict specified that people should eat fruit and vegetables for every meal if they were available.

It is understandable that there are few recipes for this produce in the kitchen records of either the monasteries or noble households. Parchment and paper were expensive, and were used only to record anything new or of interest or importance to the family. It is also understandable that during the Middle Ages, when the woman of the house alone was responsible for all domestic matters, the lines between food stuffs and medicinal products were blurred. There were very few diagnostic and therapeutic medicinal products, the hygienic conditions in the growing towns were terrible, and fear of cholera and plague, which decimated one-third of villages and sometimes half of the towns, promoted superstition and belief in magic.

The "wise women" or "old wives" were the older women of the peasant community who preserved the local folklore and practiced medicine with secret herbal remedies that were handed down from mother to daughter. Generation upon generation of peasant children learned to gather healing herbs from the woods, meadows, and streams, and to guard the secret of where they grew. In this way a knowledge of herbs and their uses, which had been developing since prehistoric times, was preserved and protected.

ON THE FIRE

In the early Middle Ages food was cooked over an open fire. Typical cooking pots were large iron or copper kettles, which were hung on chains that could be swung out over the fire or drawn back, and capacious cauldrons, sturdy pots on three legs in which all the food was cooked slowly over the glowing coals on a tripod or in the tiled oven. Although there are records of splendid meals enjoyed by the noble and merchant classes, most people had much simpler fare. The stockpot was the main source of all meals, the contents being added to and varying daily according to what was available. The meaty flavor of chicken or hare might

Garlic came originally from central Asia and was a popular herb in the Middle Ages, as can be seen in this illustration from the housekeeping book of the Cerruti family.

linger for days after the last slivers of meat itself had been eaten, while the substance was provided by dried vegetables from the previous harvest, beans, chestnuts, turnips, and wild

herbs from the forests and meadows, or cultivated herbs from the garden.

At this time spices were expensive and scarce, and therefore used only in the food of the nobility and merchant classes. They were used to enhance flavor or offset saltiness in some dishes, as well as to provide interest to combinations of different types of meat that were first boiled, then roasted until they had lost all their own taste. Later, when improved cultivation methods and the cornucopia of new plants from the New World provided more varied and better quality foods, methods of cooking changed. Spices were no longer intended to deaden and deceive the taste-buds, but were supposed to indicate the true flavor of meat, fish, and vegetables. A new simplicity was born. Cabbage was supposed to taste like cabbage, leek like leek, and the introduction of clear, light bouillon, a reduced meat stock seasoned with herbs, was a sensation. Herbs, which were once the mainstay of the peasant meal, were, and have remained, fashionable, while the blossoming trade with eastern Asia eventually led to spices becoming commonplace and finding their way onto the tables of ordinary citizens.

THE KITCHEN GARDEN — A TIMELESS EXAMPLE

The Roman courtyard garden and the monastery garden survived the dissolution of the monasteries after the Reformation as examples of an herb garden. In the course of time the kitchen garden has developed its own rules. But even if garlic and shallots do not line the borders to keep pests away from the green herbs, or if roses are no longer planted there for spiced wine, the herb garden is usually still sited close to the house, perhaps protected from birds and other animals by netting or a fence, so that the cook has only to step out of the kitchen to pick lemon balm for the salad or marjoram for the vegetable stew.

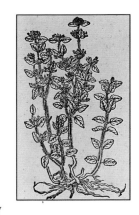

Woodcut of wild basil, in Eicones Plantarum *by the German botanist Tabernaemontanus (Frankfurt am Main, 1590).*

A GUIDE TO CULINARY HERBS

Books on cooking started with the first encyclopedias of culinary herbs. Wherever tablets thousands of years old are found, whenever former libraries are discovered, they always include lists and descriptions of herbs. Why did herbs become so important at such an early date? People gathered leaves and berries even before they began to eat raw meat. Perhaps they found that the leaves of plants improved the taste of the meat, both in its raw state and, later, after the discovery of fire, when they learned to cook it. Right from the start there seems to have been more than just one herb being used. Herbs often gave a new, improved flavor to simple ingredients, and also alleviated the stomachache caused by the monotonous and coarse food. In other ingredients, which, later, were cooked in fire-pits, they brought out the full flavor for the first time. Was this magic? The wise "old wives" certainly noticed how many different herbs grew by the roadside and in the woods, and how differently they smelled and tasted. They confirmed and extended the list of healing and tasty herbs each year, making their knowledge part of the oral tradition, until mages and monks recorded and described the facts that for many years had been part of the culinary lore of housewives of the time. What the authors themselves did not know, they invented, and what was little more than theory or superstition often was treated as fact. It is only in modern times that we have acquired a scientifically accurate knowledge of herbs.

The following chapter is a guide to the green paradise you can create for yourself. It includes familiar plants as well as some that may be less well known, and groups them together by similarity of taste or use. Because the common names of herbs may vary from place to place, the Latin botanical names are also given.

Many herbs may look very similar. **Do not use plants picked in the wild unless you are absolutely sure you have correctly identified a variety that is safe for human consumption.**

THE GARLIC FAMILY

Garlic (*Allium sativum*), a relative of the onion and one of the oldest cultivated plants, is a native of central Asia. Today it is grown throughout the world, but particularly in Asia, the Mediterranean countries, and California. The little town of Gilroy in the Santa Clara Valley, California, the biggest closed cultivation area in the world, celebrates its status as the center of the garlic world every year.

This fresh red garlic from Nepal is known as alio turco. A fresh herb available in spring, it spans the gap until winter produce is available later in the year.

Fresh white garlic has a more delicate and milder taste than dried garlic. The juicy green stalks tell you the garlic is fresh. Fresh garlic can be kept only for a limited period.

Dried garlic, whether red (as shown here) or white, generally does not differ much from type to type. However, both special mild and strong varieties are available.

Smoked garlic has a mild smoky taste. It can be used whenever you want to add a smoky flavor to a dish.

Botanically, garlic is a perennial, but under cultivation it becomes an annual. It has long, narrow leaves, which are generally droopy. The flower stalk can grow to 3 ft high and bears a spherical, reddish-white flower. The edible part of the plant consists of a round parent bulb with fifteen or more smaller bulbs. These are made up of thick, white leaves that are positioned very close to each other as a result of compression of the buds at the base of the plant. Each of these leaves encloses three to five small bulbs, which are known as cloves. Every blunt-ended, fleshy clove is surrounded by a thin skin, which, depending on the variety, can be white, purple, or reddish.

The intense, strong taste and smell are caused by sulfur-containing compounds. After people have eaten even a tiny amount of garlic their breath and skin give off the scent. This side effect, which can be unpleasant, once made garlic unpopular; nowadays both mild garlic, such as so-called elephant garlic, as well as stronger types are available. If you like the taste of garlic but do not want your skin or breath to smell of it, you can try one of the countless traditional preventive measures recommended in old wives' tales, from drinking freshly squeezed lemon juice, eating whole cloves, parsley, fennel, or honey, to drinking a glass of milk or red wine after the meal.

In addition to sulfur-bearing essential oils, garlic contains vitamins A, B, and C as well as elements that have antibacterial properties. Garlic detoxifies the body, because it is able to flush out heavy metals through the kidneys. It also reduces blood pressure, strengthens the coronary vessels and can appreciably reduce the cholesterol level as well as the level of other fats in the bloodstream.

Garlic is sold fresh (in this case the stalks are green and the outer skin of the bulb is still fresh), semi-dried (the stalk and outer skin are not completely dry) and dried (the outer skin of the bulb and the skin around each clove are completely dry). There also are a number of products made from dried garlic: garlic salt, granules, and flakes. Garlic salt can contain more than 90 percent table salt and up to 10 percent garlic. You can also get freeze-dried garlic and garlic paste or purée.

At home fresh garlic should be kept cool and dry, but not in the refrigerator. As a general principle, the younger the cloves, the milder the taste. More mature garlic is stronger, but as soon as it begins to sprout, it loses the typical, powerful garlic taste.

Dried garlic is often made into braids in France and Italy. In Polesine, near Rovigo in Italy, garlic grows in huge fields. At harvest time the plants are simply pulled out of the ground and left to dry for eight to ten days in the blazing sun. The garlic is then kept at 34°F in a cold store until it is needed, when it is taken out and braided.

Garlic plants form leaves with pointed tips up to a 3 ft in length.

○ Kitchen know-how

Rarely do opinions on herbs and spices differ as much as they do on the question of whether or not garlic tastes good. Garlic goes well with most meats, particularly lamb and mutton. It can be rubbed into large roasts, or crushed or very finely chopped for use in stews and bean recipes, and imparts its flavor to salads if it is rubbed around the inside of the salad bowl. If you do not want to crush or chop garlic, you can cook whole, unpeeled cloves, which will lend a delicate flavor to the food. The longer garlic cooks, the milder it tastes. When roasting or frying, however, it burns easily and then will taste bitter. Throughout the Mediterranean there are many recipes that owe their characteristic taste to garlic: Macedonian lamb stew, pesto alla genovese, aïoli, gazpacho, soupe au pistou, baked garlic, and pommes Provençale. Asian cooking also relies on garlic, which lends a healthy background bite to many recipes. Wherever olive oil is pressed, garlic is preserved in it, either on its own or with other spices. In Tuscany garlic cloves are traditionally seasoned with peppercorns and bay leaves (as shown here). In Greece, on the other hand, rosemary, thyme, and lemon peel are added.

Crow garlic (*Allium vineale*) grows in vineyards in southern and central Europe. The bulbs are used in the same way as garlic. The leaves can be used too, but only as a garnish. **Bear's garlic**(*Allium ursinum*), also known as ramsons, is a native of Europe, North America and northern Asia, and is noticeable for its intense, garlic-like aroma. It is rarely cultivated but is usually found in shaded locations on damp, humus-rich floors of deciduous forests. Its large leaves are similar to those of the poisonous lily-of-the-valley, but give off a strong scent of garlic. Both the fresh leaves and the bulbs —

Garlic in a Thai market *In Asia many different varieties of garlic are available, from the familiar white and red to head garlic.*

Head garlic *is a Thai speciality. The tiny garlic cloves grow on the stalk instead of a flower. They are used raw in spicy pickled foods and with steamed shrimp.*

Crow garlic. *The shiny, silvery, delicate bulbs have a pleasant garlic flavor with a slightly bitter overtone.*

To prepare garlic

Start at the root and peel away the hard skin, working from the top to the bottom.

The core should be removed from more mature cloves because it usually tastes astringent and bitter. To do this, slice the clove in half lengthwise first.

Crush the cloves with a broad-bladed knife. This is a good method to use if you want to chop lots of small cloves quickly.

An easy alternative to chopping garlic is to use a garlic press, which works even if some of the skin is still stuck to the cloves.

○ Kitchen know-how

Regional Asian cooks are particularly skilled in their use of garlic. Although the various varieties of garlic are used in large quantities and in a great many recipes, the persistent taste and smell is not as noticeable as in Balkan specialities, for example, or those from the Near East. It is considered a great skill, in the spicy cuisine of the Chinese province of Szechuan, for example, to be able to "hide" the garlic, in other words to use it so subtly in seasoning that it enhances the overall flavor of the dish without being noticeable itself. There is scarcely a recipe in Thailand and Indochina that does not use at least a small quantity. However, it is particularly important in hot chili specialities, where it is mostly used in conjunction with basil for a contrast in flavor. This also includes the hot sauces from Southeast Asia, where garlic, together with shrimp paste, compensates for the heat of the chilies.

which are similar to those of garlic — are used in cooking. **Chives** (*Allium schoenoprasum*) are a perennial plant found throughout the world. They are cultivated intensively by commercial growers and can also be grown easily in herb gardens, patio tubs, and flowerpots. The green, hollow, smooth leaves taste like leeks and onions, and have a remarkably high vitamin C content. The leaves, which grow back after they are cut, are gathered from the fields throughout the summer; in winter chives come from greenhouses, where they are grown primarily as potted plants. Chives are harvested before they flower, because afterwards much of the flavor is lost. They can be kept for a long time if deep frozen. There are three varieties, which are distinguished by the thickness of the leaves: fine, medium-fine, and wide-tubed. **Perennial Chinese chives** (*Allium tuberosum*) grow wild in China, Japan, and northern India, and are cultivated throughout Southeast Asia and in California. In general the plant is larger than chives, and has thick, dry leaves that are not hollow, but flat. Occasionally the name Chinese chives is also used for the variety *Allium odorum*, which is native to most of Asia. Despite it name, **Welsh onion** (*Allium fistulosum*) is thought be native to central and western China. It is a winter green, which, with its thickened illusory phylum (the flower stems are thickened), appears similar to leek and can be gathered throughout the year. There are many cultivated forms in Asia, including red-stemmed varieties, which are used widely in cooking. The **shallot** (*Allium cepa* var. *proliferum*, syn. *Allium ascalonicum*), sometimes called the tree onion, does not flower but forms spicy offshoot bulbs, which are used in cooking. **Rocambole** (*Allium sativum* var. *ophioscordum*) is perennial and grows to 3 ft high with bulbs that are like garlic but have fewer cloves. Instead of the whitish-green flowers, it is mainly offshoot bulbs that form on the frail plant.

Bear's garlic *covers large areas of damp woodland in spring. Because of its smell it cannot be confused with poisonous lily-of-the-valley leaves, which have no scent.*

Bear's garlic *produces two lanceolate leaves up to 10 in. long. The white flowers, which look like umbels, flower in late spring.*

○ Kitchen know-how

Bear's garlic is very similar in taste and smell to garlic and can be even stronger. As it is not cultivated, the time to use it is spring, when it can be found in woods. Herb butter made with bear's garlic is a refreshing, hearty spread for bread. Bear's garlic can be used raw to season soup and vegetables, or as a component of salads; when boiled, it is an alternative to spinach. The sometimes strong smell of raw bear's garlic is transformed during cooking into a mild, garlicky aroma. Bear's garlic bulbs can be chopped or crushed and used in the same way as garlic cloves.

Garlic baked in red wine: *fresh young bulbs are baked whole. The cloves can then be squeezed out and the contents eaten on bread with salt, or the garlic can be puréed and served as an accompaniment to meat or vegetables.*

Bear's garlic *is a close relative of garlic. The leaves should only be used fresh; when boiled or dried they lose a lot of their taste.*

Several species of **Allium** *are sold in Asian markets as popular everyday herbs. The leaves and flowers of Chinese chives are added to all kinds of dishes in the same way as chives or garlic. The leaves taste and smell strongly of garlic, but the aroma dissipates quickly. There is also a bleached variety of green Chinese chives, shown on the left, with white flowers. It is grown in the dark, which prevents the formation of green chlorophyll. As a result, the bleached Chinese chives have a more delicate, milder taste. However, they will keep for only two days, even if stored in the refrigerator.*

○ Kitchen know-how

The leaves of many varieties of *Allium* have been used throughout the ages in Asian cooking. **Chinese chives** are particularly popular, because they have a taste between that of garlic and chives. Whether green or bleached, the flat leaves, which are also similar to leek, are favored for use in wok recipes, omelets and other egg dishes. A strongly flavored Thai cake is filled with Chinese chives and called, not surprisingly, "Chinese chive cake". The taste of the herb also combines well with mung beans and thread noodles. **Chives** taste spicy and fresh, like onion. They are useful in any dish where a fresh onion flavor is required. The leaves are finely snipped and added to the food after preparation. Chives should not be chopped or mashed, because it makes them quickly lose their flavor, and they should not be subjected to heat, because then they lose their vitamins.. They have many different uses as a garnish. **Welsh onions** are most popular in the Far East, particularly in Japan, where dozens of varieties are available. They are often bleached, which gives them a more delicate taste.

Chinese leek *is also known as large-leafed chives. The plant is bigger and the leaves are wider than those of chives, and the flavor is somewhat stronger. Like its relatives, Chinese leek should be used fresh and is not suitable for drying.*

Nira, *a variety of Chinese chives popular in Japan, have a taste somewhere in between garlic and chives. The dark green leaves are best. The younger, shorter leaves are milder and more delicate. Nira is a popular herb for use in egg roll fillings.*

Chinese chives *can be used instead of garlic. In Asia they are valued for use in stir-frys and as an accompaniment to fish. The flower stems with the closed white flower buds, which have a honey-like flavor, are considered a delicacy.*

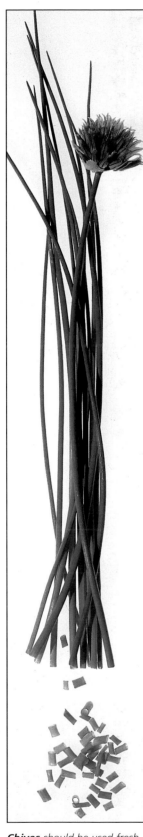

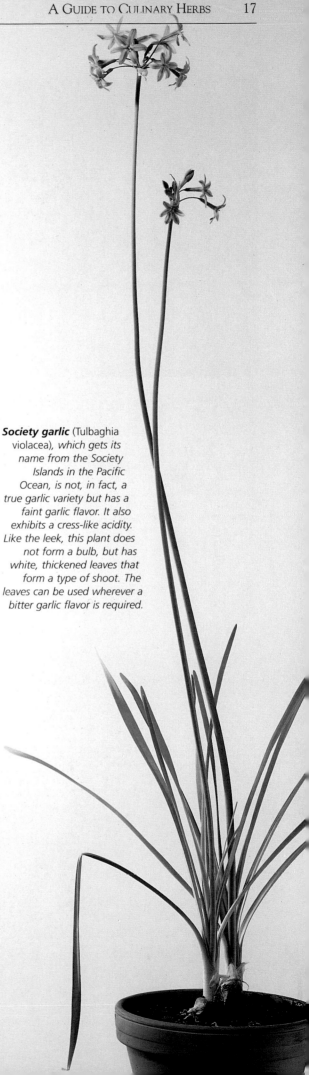

Society garlic (Tulbaghia violacea), *which gets its name from the Society Islands in the Pacific Ocean, is not, in fact, a true garlic variety but has a faint garlic flavor. It also exhibits a cress-like acidity. Like the leek, this plant does not form a bulb, but has white, thickened leaves that form a type of shoot. The leaves can be used wherever a bitter garlic flavor is required.*

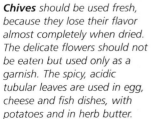

Chives *should be used fresh, because they lose their flavor almost completely when dried. The delicate flowers should not be eaten but used only as a garnish. The spicy, acidic tubular leaves are used in egg, cheese and fish dishes, with potatoes and in herb butter.*

Welsh onion *is often confused with Italian rocambole. The tubular leaves, which taste like onion and chives, are used primarily as a seasoning, while the moderately large bulb can be used as an alternative to scallions.*

Rocambole *is sometimes also known as gourmet garlic because of its delicate taste. Every part of this small, exceedingly delicate variety of garlic can be used in cooking, even the little offshoot bulbs that develop on the flower stems.*

DILL AND FENNEL

Fennel (*Foeniculum vulgare*) is a hardy herbaceous perennial that is native to the Mediterranean and Asia Minor and now is grown throughout the world in temperate zones. It has a bulbous, many-headed root, from which numerous grooved stems grow. It can grow to a height of 6 ft and has yellow umbellate flowers. The long-stemmed, blue-green, feathery, thread-like leaves are similar to dill leaves in appearance, but taste completely different. The leaves can be harvested throughout the summer, along with the stems. Fennel can be used to aid digestion, as a sedative, and as an antispasmodic. Fennel the herb is closely related to fennel the vegetable (*Foeniculum dulce*), also called Florence fennel and finocchio. The thick, fleshy leaves and bulbous root of this vegetable can be cooked or used raw in salads. Dill (*Anethum graveolens*), an annual that can be found growing wild in Europe and in North and South America, is now cultivated worldwide. It has a thin tap root from which a grooved stem grows to over 3 ft in height, bearing very fine feathery, delicate leaves all around the stalks. Dill leaves are much more delicate than those of fennel. The seeds are also used as a spice because, like the rest of the plant, they contain essential oils. Dill is cultivated intensively to supply the greengrocery trade and is usually gathered when it has reached a height of 7–12 in. When used for pickling gherkins the plants are harvested at a height of 15–23 in. just before they flower. Fresh dill cannot be kept for long before it wilts. It is necessary to use greater quantities of dried dill than fresh, because dried dill loses its flavor. Frozen dill retains both its flavor and aroma. In antiquity dill, like fennel, aniseed, and caraway, was considered an important medicinal plant because it has a soothing effect. In homeopathic medicine dill is used to strengthen the stomach and relieve flatulence.

After the yellow umbellate flowers open, dill produces deeply grooved, yellowish-brown to yellowish-gray seeds, which look like caraway. The seeds are used mainly in France and Italy to flavor bread and cakes. Fennel is grown primarily for the seeds; as an herb it is only of secondary importance. Wild fennel, also known as Sicilian or Italian fennel, does not have the same strong aniseed taste and cannot be compared with herb fennel. In Sicily it is used to season fresh sardines.

Fennel leaves have a pleasant aromatic, sweetish, and slightly astringent taste, like aniseed. They can be used in dishes where the seeds are also used. In Provence dried fennel stems are mixed with charcoal to lend barbecued food a distinctive flavor.

Delicate dill leaves are just the thing when subtle seasoning is required. Fresh dill has a very delicate, slightly tangy flavor, which cannot be compared with any other herb, not even with closely related aniseed and caraway. It is used fresh, rather than added during cooking, to preserve its intense flavor.

At this commercial dill field at Albenga on the Ligurian coast in Italy the herb is harvested before it flowers and is tied into bunches by skilled workers. The bunches are transported upright in special packaging lined with water-soaked sponges to keep the Scandinavian market supplied with its favorite herb.

○ Kitchen know-how

Dill is closely associated with the national cuisines of Scandinavia and the Baltic states, and has also been popularized elsewhere by immigrants from these countries. A good example of dill as a superb seasoning is gravadlax (salmon marinated in coarse sea salt and lots of dill). Combinations of acidic ingredients and sugar bring out the best in dill's flavor, which is why they are used in so many marinades for fish and vegetables, in pickled herrings, mustard, and flavored vinegar. In Finland even forest fruits are preserved in a sweet and sour mixture and heavily flavored with dill. In Scandinavia when a dish is garnished with dill, you do not get just a couple of sprigs, but a whole bunch. Even the simple "poor man's cuisine" in Scandinavia and throughout eastern and central Europe has dill to thank for spicing up the staple dish of potatoes in white sauce.

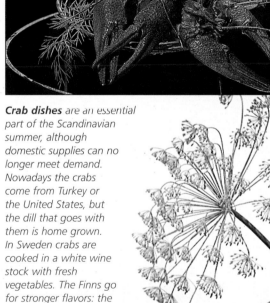

Crab dishes are an essential part of the Scandinavian summer, although domestic supplies can no longer meet demand. Nowadays the crabs come from Turkey or the United States, but the dill that goes with them is home grown. In Sweden crabs are cooked in a white wine stock with fresh vegetables. The Finns go for stronger flavors: the stock is made of vinegar and beer, with salt, plenty of sugar and lots of dill.

During the cucumber season dill crowns, the traditional herb used for pickling cucumbers, are also widely available.

From the yellow umbellate flowers come dill seeds, which can be used fresh or dried. The seeds taste stronger than the herb and are reminiscent of caraway.

ANGELICA AND CAMOMILE

At harvest time vast quantities of camomile flowers are available, as shown here in Barcelona. In cooking camomile is used mainly as a flavoring in sweet dishes, and its oil is used in salads. It is chiefly used in homeopathy.

Angelica (*Angelica archangelica*) is a hardy plant that flourishes in damp meadows and on the banks of rivers in Scandinavia, central Europe, Asia, and America. The plant grows to 9 ft in height and has a sweetish aroma. The large double or triple pinnate leaves branch off all around the stem, which is thick, hollow, and slightly grooved. The plant forms a strong head of flowers with yellow-green double umbels that are almost spherical. The tap roots and grooved seeds are used to make liqueurs such as Benedictine and Chartreuse, and the seeds are also used in some perfumes. Angelica aids digestion, is valued for its stomach-strengthening properties, and is used to treat anemia and cold symptoms. It was formerly used as a plague preventive. When candied, the stem is used to decorate cakes and pastries. The finely snipped or chopped leaves can be used in fruit desserts or with fish dishes. Care should be taken when harvesting the stalk and leaves, because the sap can cause skin irritations. **Camomile**(*Chamaemelum nobile*, syn. *Anthemis nobilis*) is a perennial that can be found growing wild in Europe and North America. Both the leaves and the daisy-like flowers (the white petals are folded back further) are dried for use. The flowers smell slightly of apple. Camomile oil is used in cooking only in salads. It is known that a decoction of camomile flowers will settle the stomach. In folk medicine camomile is considered an all-around treatment. It prevents inflammation, is an antispasmodic, promotes healing, and is useful as a gargle, for poultices, and as a rinse.

Angelica. The hollow stems of angelica have a spicy or bitter, acidic taste. When preserved in sugar, the acidity and bitterness are transformed into a perfumed, fresh and spicy flavor. Candied angelica is used as a decoration for cakes, especially petits fours *and* pralines.

Young angelica leaves, with their powerful taste — spicy-sweet at first, then bitter and acidic — add a special flavor to salads. If the slightly sweet stalks are cooked with rhubarb or other acidic fruit, they lessen the acidic taste and thus reduce the need for sugar.

WOODRUFF

Woodruff (*Asperula odorata*) is a hardy plant that grows wild in northern and central Europe, and from North Africa across the Balkans to Siberia. It is cultivated in North America. The square stalk grows up to 12 in. high, with six to eight solid, lanceolate leaves positioned at different points in a circle around the stem. The herb is harvested before it flowers and is used fresh or dried. The typical aroma of coumarin develops only when the leaves have wilted or been dried. In some countries the use of woodruff is discouraged because in large quantities it can be dangerous to health. Bunches of woodruff stored in a linen closet will keep moths at bay. In herbal medicine the plant is used as an infusion for its calming and sleep-inducing effect.

Woodruff is spicy and bitter, and in cooking it is generally used in conjunction with sugar, which emphasizes its taste. It is used to flavor sweet dishes and in May punch with white wine and Champagne.

Woodruff grows in shaded mixed woods. When freshly picked, it is easy to freeze. For this purpose it is best to pack the leaves and stems loosely in foil containers rather than tied in bunches. They can then be used in the same way as the fresh herb.

OYSTER PLANT AND GARDEN MACE

The oyster plant (*Mertensia maritima*) should not be confused with salsify (*Trapopogon porrifolius*), which is sometimes called by this name. It is closely related to borage and comes from the northern coast of Scotland. It grows on salty ground and prefers a high level of humidity. The creeping stems bear blue-green, oval, smooth, succulent, very delicate stemmed leaves and decorative blue flowers. **Garden mace** (*Achillea decolorans*) is closely related to the milfoil (*Achillea millefolium*), which has been used as a healing plant since time immemorial. Garden mace can be called the herb version of milfoil. The herbaceous perennial grows in damp, semi-shaded places. The cream-colored flowers bloom throughout the summer. Only the tender, fresh leaves are used as a flavoring in cooking.

CHERVIL

Chervil (*Anthriscus cerefolium*) is a native of southeast Europe, western Asia and southern Russia that now grows throughout Europe and North America. Botanically, chervil, an annual that can grow to 2 ft high, is closely related to parsley and carrot. It has two to four pinnate leaves, which are soft and smooth on top but very hairy on the underside. The fresh leaves are used as an herb and are harvested before flowering because old leaves have little taste. The thin stems can be eaten and the flowers are also used, as long as they are still closed. Frozen leaves lose their rigidity. As a medicinal plant, chervil acts as a blood purifier and diuretic. It is also claimed that chervil, which should be added at the end of the cooking time, increases the flavor of other herbs.

The oyster plant has an unusually delicate flavor that really is reminiscent of oysters and therefore is ideally suited to substantial dishes. The slightly salty, spicy taste works particularly well in fresh salads and with any raw fruit and vegetables. The leaves can also be used in sandwiches.

Chervil is a typical spring herb. The fine, slightly aniseed taste goes well with fish, potatoes, and, of course, with salads. It cannot be used dried. Because of its appearance chervil is often mistaken for parsley, but the leaves are a paler green, smaller and more filigreed, and the aroma is rather more delicate.

○ Kitchen know-how

The delicate, fresh and slightly sweet, aniseed aroma and flavor of chervil is reminiscent of parsley, with which it is often combined to extremely good effect. In addition to chives and tarragon, chervil is an indispensable ingredient in the French *fines herbes* mixture, which should be added only at the end of cooking time. Chervil is used in soups because it stimulates the appetite. In the soup pictured here, shallots and diced onions are sweated in melted butter until transparent, then simmered with a selection of finely chopped stock vegetables, such as carrots, celery, and cabbage. The soup is then seasoned with chervil, puréed, strained through a sieve and the flavor adjusted with fresh cream. Chervil can also be used as garnish, but the leaves wilt faster than those of parsley. Sometimes chervil is preserved in vinegar or oil.

Garden mace is still generally unknown in many areas. You can try to grow it if you can find a source for the seeds, or see if it is available in specialist shops. It has tender leaves that are only vaguely reminiscent of nutmeg. They taste spicy, slightly salty, and acidic, and are delicious in fresh salads.

TARRAGON

Tarragon (*Artemisia dracunculus*), a perennial plant growing to 6 ft high, originated in southern Russia and was supposedly brought by the Crusaders from Asia Minor to Europe, where it quickly established itself in the monastery gardens. Today tarragon is found from Siberia to North America and is cultivated mainly in France and Italy. The strong, woody roots form runners under the ground, from which grow bushy, branching stems with narrow, non-pinnate leaves about 2 in. in length. Panicles form at the tips, with small, inconspicuous yellow-green flowers. There are two types of tarragon. Genuine **French tarragon** (*Artemisia dracunculus*) is prized in *haute cuisine* and by lovers of French cooking for its delicate aroma and taste. It is spicy and refreshing, with a slightly sweet aftertaste, and is never bitter. **Russian tarragon** (*Artemisia dracunculoides*) has narrower, paler, and hairy leaves. It tastes drier, more bitter, and slightly unctuous, and

Béarnaise sauce is a good example of the happy marriage between French tarragon and white wine. A reduction of white wine, wine vinegar, shallots, tarragon, and chervil is beaten together with egg yolks and butter, then seasoned to taste with more tarragon and white wine. Tarragon combines well with vinegar, mustard, and any acidic taste.

Tarragon is a typical single herb with a very individual aroma. Used in large quantities, it particularly enhances the flavor of onions and shallots.

○ Kitchen know-how

French tarragon has ensured a permanent place for itself in the gastronomic world as a component in *fines herbes* with chervil and chives. The delicate spicy taste stands out well, and the full flavor develops during cooking, for example, in chicken with tarragon. Both French and Russian tarragon are favored for use in butters, mayonnaise, mustard, and vinegar. It is often used with dill and parsley. If you want to combine tarragon with other herbs, use it sparingly so that its distinctive taste is not too dominant.

stimulates the appetite. In cooking, tarragon leaves and the young shoots are used. Because tarragon wilts as soon as it is picked, it is worth always having fresh tarragon available at home — it will grow in the garden, in a greenhouse or flowerpot, and should be picked immediately before use. When dried, tarragon loses some of the volatile aromatics and thus some of its taste. In industrial production powerful aromatic tarragon oil is used. While in antiquity tarragon was carried on the person to prevent snake bites (hence the Latin name *dracunculus* — small dragon, snake), it is now used as a proven diuretic and digestive stimulant.

__Mugwort__ promotes the digestion of fat and is therefore recommended for use with fatty meats such as goose, duck, and pork. The delicate, dry aroma, which is reminiscent of mint and juniper, is displayed at its best with these dishes.

__Hops__ (Humulus lupulus) were crowned king of the mugwort family in the eighth century for their role as a flavoring and preservative in beer.

__Sea mugwort__ (Artemisia maritima), with its delicately proportioned leaves, forms a silver-gray carpet along the salt meadows of the North Sea coast. Its aroma is more subtle than that of mugwort, and is similar to that of curry. It can be used in the same way as mugwort.

MUGWORT, SOUTHERNWOOD AND WORMWOOD

Mugwort (*Artemisia vulgaris*) is a perennial plant originating in Europe, North America and central Asia, which grows to 6 ft high, and is cultivated throughout almost the entire world. The leaves, which are dark green and smooth on top and felty white underneath, as well as the tips of sprays with unopened buds, are sold fresh or dried, usually rubbed, but sometimes also ground. Mugwort has a diuretic and antispasmodic effect. **Southernwood** (*Artemisia abrotanum*), or lad's love, is a bushy perennial shrub that grows to 5 ft high and is a native of the Near East and southeastern Europe, and can be found in North America. Its delicate pinnate leaves, which are smooth on the surface and coarsely haired underneath, lend a special flavor to sauces and roast meats. Southernwood is good for stomach upsets and coughs, and an infusion made from its leaves is reputed to expel roundworms from humans and animals. **Wormwood** (*Artemisia absinthium*), a strongly scented perennial plant, is native to southern Europe, North Africa, and Asia. Both stems and leaves are covered in a close, fine, silver-gray coating of hairs. The essential oil contained in wormwood, thujon, is dangerous and can be used only in small quantities. In the form of bitters it is an appetite stimulant, an antispasmodic, and a sedative.

__When first tasted,__ southernwood seems very similar to lemon balm. But then the peppery-bitter flavor, which is reminiscent of mugwort but more delicate, comes through. Southernwood can be used, sparingly, in preparing beef, pork, and eel.

__Wormwood__ is an extremely bitter herb. It is hardly ever used as a seasoning, except in fatty pork roasts and lamb dishes. The bitter elements aid digestion. It is important for the production of liqueurs and aromatized wines.

Borage has bright blue flowers, which
are used, fresh or candied, as a
garnish for cold platters, salads, and
punch bowls. Vinegar turns blue if
borage flowers are added to it.

BORAGE AND CAPERS

Borage (*Borago officinalis*) is native to the eastern
Mediterranean, but now grows wild throughout almost
all of Europe and is cultivated in many countries. From
its rosette of leaves this annual plant grows up to 3 ft in
height, with bright azure blue, drooping star-shaped
flowers. While the stem is coarsely haired, almost
brush-like, the young oval-shaped leaves, which are
covered in hairs on both sides, feel almost velvety, but
older leaves are hard and rough. The edible flowers are
arranged as double sprays at the end of the stems. In
cooking, the young leaves can be used fresh or frozen,
rubbed or ground. The fresh leaves are most strongly
scented, and, as they wilt quickly, they should be
picked shortly before use. The plant contains mucilage,
and is effective as a cardiotonic, calmative, and blood
purifier. It is recommended for coughs and depression,
and promotes the release of adrenaline. Its name can be
attributed to this function: it is derived from *borrach*,
the Celtic word for courage, and refers to the stirring
feelings imparted by the consumption of its leaves.
Capers (*Capparis spinosa*) are the closed, preserved
buds of the caper plant, which is cultivated in the
Mediterranean. This shrub forms branches up to 13 ft
in length, and has oval, thick leaves, with the
secondary leaves forming thorns. The long-stemmed,
olive to dark green buds are located in the crux of the
leaves and are harvested by hand before they open.
After a short wilting process they are salted and
partially preserved in vinegar or oil. The salting process
lends the normally bland caper its typical acidic to dry
and spicy flavor. Capers must always be kept covered
and immersed in liquid, but neither vinegar nor oil
should be added to already preserved capers. Capers
should not be cooked but added to hot dishes just
before serving. The flavor depends on the size: the
bigger the caper, the stronger the flavor. As a general
rule, good capers of any size should be firm. In healing,
capers are used for spleen problems.

○ Kitchen know-how

Borage is really a summer herb, because its spicy, slightly
bitter flavor, reminiscent of cucumber, is best when fresh.
The furry leaves are not suitable for drying, but can be
frozen, preferably finely chopped. Borage goes with all
types of herbs and in dishes using eels, and both leaves
and flowers can be used in salads instead of cucumber. It
can also be prepared in the same way as spinach
(although some of the flavor is lost if it is boiled), or be
added to turnip and spinach as a flavoring. Borage adds a
refreshing flavor to a variety of drinks.

○ Kitchen know-how

Strictly speaking, capers are not an herb but a spice.
However, since they are usually combined with fresh
herbs they are included in this book. Salted capers, with
the unmistakable "caper flavor", are a part of everyday
cookery in the Mediterranean area, where they are used
to season fish, tender veal, rabbit, and poultry. If you are
preparing an authentic Italian or Spanish dish, you
should never use capers preserved in vinegar, but salted
capers, which may be available in Italian delicatessens.
As a compromise, you can use capers preserved in oil.
Capers are also used to season dishes suited to acidic
flavors, such as cold meats and pickled foods.

Harvesting capers in Salina, one of the Liparian islands off the north coast of Sicily. The buds are gathered around the time of the summer solstice.

If the caper bud is not picked, it develops into a fabulous flower. However, the airy splendor lasts for only one day.

Each morning the buds are stripped from the branches one by one, a hard manual job. Only buds that are the right size are collected.

The fruit that develops from the blossom is highly prized by gourmets in southern Europe, and is usually sold as a preserve. Outside the Mediterranean countries where it is grown, however, it is largely unknown. It has a very spicy taste and can be served in the same way as, and with, pickled olives. In Spain these fruits are classified according to four sizes: finos ($1/2$ in.), medianos extra ($1/2 - 2/3$ in.), medianos ($2/3 - 3/4$ in.) and gruesos (over $3/4$ in.). As with capers, the smaller the fruit, the finer the quality.

The best quality capers are handpicked. In this way crushed buds and ones that have opened are removed before the capers are left to dry overnight.

Salted capers are, unfortunately, usually available only in the Mediterranean countries. When preserved in this way they are much more aromatic than when packed in vinegar.

Nonpareilles   **Surfines**   **Fines**   **Milfines**   **Capucines**   **Capottes**

The smallest are the best. This has become the rule for capers, but it does not mean that the bigger ones are less spicy. Classification into different sizes and the names given to them are not uniform. Commercially, the French classifications are generally used. The largest capers are called Communes.

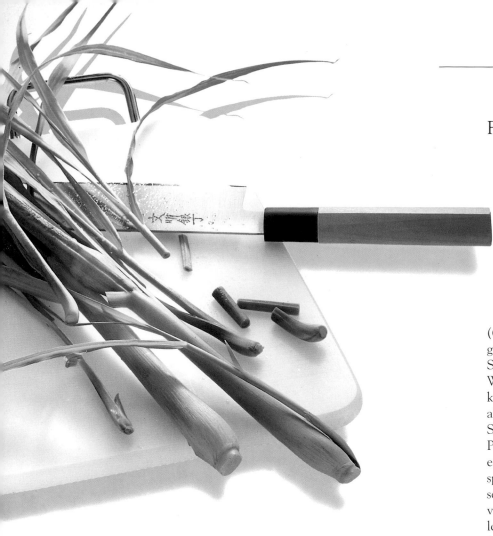

○ Kitchen know-how

Lemon grass is used as a spice in many soups, especially fish soup, and in sauces, crab and meat dishes, curries, salads, vegetables, drinks and sweet dishes throughout Southeast Asia. It is also used in the manufacture of liqueurs. The taste complements those of garlic, onion, chili and fresh cilantro. The leaves are cut into pieces $^3/_4$ in. long and cooked with the food, then removed just before serving. **Citronella grass** has a very similar, but sharper lemon taste.

Lemon grass *grows throughout the tropical belt. It is used in regional cooking, especially in Thai and Indonesian dishes.*

Citronella grass *has a scent reminiscent of lemon and roses. It is used in the same way as lemon grass.*

FRESH AS A LEMON

The beguiling scent of lemons can be brought into the kitchen without having to rely on members of the citrus family. **Lemon grass** (*Cymbopogon citratus*) is an annual plant that flourishes in the tropics. Its powerful, lemon taste is due to citral, the essential oil it contains. In Southeast Asian cooking only the very bottom – about 6 in. – of the narrow raw leaves is used; this part is white and thick, and is used fresh or dried wherever a fresh lemon flavor is required. When dried and ground, it is sold as sereh powder. **Citronella grass** (*Cymbopogon nardus*) can be used instead of lemon grass; it has a similar taste and also grows in the tropics. Sri Lankan citronella oil is made from the leaves. When used in cooking, the leaves are crushed with a knife or ground in a mortar. **Kaffir lime** (*Citrus hystrix*), also known as Makrut lime, comes originally from Southeast Asia, between Sri Lanka and the Philippines. The flowers and the skin of the fruit, but especially the leaves of this little tree, are used as a spice. The tree has thin branches and small, heavily seeded, very thick-skinned, wrinkled fruit, which is not very juicy. The leaves are unusually shaped, as if two leaves had grown on top of each other. Both leaves and fruit give off a strong scent of lemon, which is very popular in Asian cuisine. **Lemon verbena** (*Lippia citriodora*, syn. *Aloysia triphylla*) is a perennial plant originating in South America, where it can grow quite tall. It is sometimes cultivated as a substitute for lemon grass. The long, pointed, pale green leaves give off a sweet scent of lemon and can be picked throughout the year. The strong, lemon-scented oil is used for cosmetics. **The pepper plant** (*Piper sarmentosum*) is a perennial plant native to Thailand, where it is very common. It grows in tropical conditions in semi-shade in damp, nutrient-rich soil. Young, underripe or just ripe leaves are used as a seasoning in numerous dishes in Southeast Asian cuisine. **Sansho** (*Zanthoxylum piperitum*) is the name of a thorny Japanese ash tree, which is often incorrectly called the Japanese pepper tree, although it is no relation to the pepper family (Piperaceae). The tree grows up to 13 ft high. The leaves and the ground husks of the spiny seeds are used to season Japanese dishes.

The Mexican tea plant (*Chenopodium ambrosoides*), also known as American wormseed, comes from Mexico and is found throughout the United States. The perennial, aromatic plant has numerous tiny flowers, which are sited in the crux of the leaves and give off a sweet lemon scent. The plant is an important ingredient in Mexican dishes, and is used to prepare a tea in the Yucatan peninsula. It prevents the intestines from becoming infected with parasites and promotes digestion. Other plants that have a lemon-like taste are lemon basil (pages 39, 41), lemon balm (page 34) and lemon thyme (page 56).

The pepper plant *is used in vegetable soups. In Thai hors d'oeuvres the raw leaves are filled with various ingredients, such as ginger, peanuts, and shrimp.*

Kaffir lime *smells strongly of lemon. The rind is used fresh or dried, whole or cut into strips. The leaves are used finely chopped, sprinkled over the food before serving.*

The Mexican tea plant *is used in Mexico in any dish based on black beans, and it is indispensable in* quesadillas — *tortillas filled with cheese.*

Sansho *is a favorite garnish in Japanese cooking. The young leaves are also known as kinome. The refreshing flavor, reminiscent of mint, adds an individual note to soups and fish dishes.*

The powerful lemon flavor *of lemon verbena is not used often enough, which is a pity, because this attractive plant is easy to maintain in the house and thus provides a ready supply of fresh leaves. It can be used in tea or as an infusion, as a flavoring in sweet dishes, and as a seasoning in meat and fish dishes, where its fresh taste excels.*

HERBS AND SPICES FROM ASIA

The screw pine (*Pandanus tectorius*), or pandanus, which provides fibers, is native to southern Asia and tropical Australia, where it grows by the sea. The narrow, shiny, sword-shaped leaves are used as a spice. In Malaysia and Indonesia the flavor is as popular for use in sweet dishes as vanilla is elsewhere. In Thai cooking the leaves are used as a protective casing for braised foods. Meat is flavored with screw pine flowers steeped in water (kewra water)

○ Kitchen know-how

Garam masala, a mixture of spices and herbs that is made up especially for each curry, is always the basis for curry dishes in Southeast Asia. Every mixture is specifically tailored to suit the main ingredient and has an individual taste. However, all curry cooks use curry leaves. Sprigs are added during cooking and produce the indescribable, unmistakable aroma associated with all curries. The same flavor is found in the fish dishes of Madras and Sri Lankan cuisine. In Malaysia, where curry leaves are also used to season vegetable dishes, they are called *kampillay*. The seafood curry from Madras illustrated above is just one example of the huge range of curries, which are usually served with boiled rice and can sometimes be extremely hot as a result of the generous use of chilies.

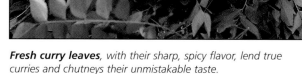

Curry leaves impart their full flavor only when they are really fresh. The only way to preserve them without losing the flavor is to freeze them.

Fresh curry leaves, with their sharp, spicy flavor, lend true curries and chutneys their unmistakable taste.

Screw pine leaves have a sweetish, aromatic taste that cannot be compared to any other spice. In Asia they are used fresh in sweet dishes, rice dishes and curries.

The very young leaves of the cardamom plant are used for seasoning. They taste similar to the fruit capsule, but are somewhat sweeter and milder.

The reed-like cardamom (*Elettaria cardamomum*), which grows up to 10 ft high, comes from the Malabar coast of India and today is cultivated there as well as in Sri Lanka and in the tropical African countries. In addition to the closed, dried and matured (in Sri Lanka, immature) oil-bearing fruits, the seeds (whole or ground) and, in Asia, the long, broad lanceolate leaves are used. Cardamom is known to be an effective treatment for strengthening the heart and stomach. **White-leaf everlasting** (*Helichrysum italicum*) is an evergreen aromatic plant from southern Europe and northwest Africa. It produces narrow, needle-like silver-gray leaves from the round white stems, which turn woody in the second year. In late summer it produces small, mustard-yellow flowers. The twigs are cooked with the leaves, but removed before serving. The aroma is reminiscent of curry mixes, although the taste is not the same. **Curry leaves** (*Murraya koenigii*) come from a small tree native to Asia, which is now cultivated in India and Africa. The green, oval leaves are paler underneath than on top. Whole sprigs are cooked in the food and removed before serving. Compared to fresh leaves, dried leaves lose a great deal of their flavor.

Vietnamese balm (*Elsholtzia ciliata*) comes from tropical and subtropical areas in Asia, and is cultivated in eastern Asia as a medicine and spice. The flowers are lavender-colored panicles. The **Chinese spice plant** (*Elsholtzia stauntonii*) is a small, hardy, slightly woody plant from China. In the Crimea it is cultivated for its essential oils. The flowers are pink. **Rau om** (*Limnophila aromatica*) is a small plant found from India to Australia. The leaves are used widely in Thai and Vietnamese cooking because of their unique flavor. **Wasabi**, or Japanese horseradish (*Eutrema wasabi*), is a perennial plant in Japan, where it has been cultivated for over a thousand years beside rivers and in cool mountainous areas. Wasabi is one of the most important seasonings in Japanese cuisine. It is primarily the barrel root, freshly grated or powdered and mixed with water, which has a penetrating, sharp flavor and is used for seasoning raw fish. Both the heart-shaped leaves and the roots are made into a mustard with rice wine. **Garland chrysanthemum** (*Chrysanthemum coronarium*) is also known as *shungiku*. It originated in the eastern Mediterranean and is cultivated in many countries. The leaves and flowers are used in oriental dishes.

White-leaf everlasting *has a sweet, mild, curry flavor. It is used in soups and vegetable dishes, rice and meat dishes.*

Rau om *tastes aromatic and slightly sweet, like cumin. It is suited to sweet and sweet-and-sour dishes.*

The Chinese spice plant *has a powerful flavor, faintly reminiscent of caraway and mint.*

Vietnamese balm *has a mild, spicy, exotic flavor, which goes well with fish dishes.*

The bitter-tasting wasabi *leaves can be used on their own as a salad.*

Garland chrysanthemum *has a slightly bitter taste, which can be alleviated by sugar or honey.*

CORIANDER

Coriander (*Coriandrum sativum*) is one of the oldest herbs known. Its name is derived from the Greek word *koris*. This annual plant is found in Europe, Asia, and the Americas. It grows first as a ground-hugging rosette with bright green, three-lobed leaves, then shoots up with strongly branching stems, with white to reddish umbelliferous flowers at the ends. The upper lobes are delicately feathered. In late summer the plant produces yellowish-brown, spherical fruit with a cleft. The seeds, the leaves – which we call cilantro – and the root are all used in cooking. Cilantro should always be used fresh. The leaves will keep if the unwashed roots are placed in water or if they are wrapped in damp paper towels and placed in the refrigerator. In herbal medicine coriander seed is successfully used for stomach and intestinal upsets. **Vietnamese coriander** (*Polygonum odoratum*) is a vigorous climbing plant. **Fitweed** (*Eryngium foetidum*), a relative of coriander from Thailand, is a major culinary herb throughout Asia and is similar to sea holly (*Eryngium maritimum*). It forms numerous little plants from the main shoot. The leaves are gathered with the stems, or the whole stem is cut off at ground level using a sharp knife. **Vap ca** (*Houttuynia cordata*) is a tropical plant native to Vietnam. It prefers damp or wet locations, and forms numerous runners. **Sea arrowgrass** (*Triglochin maritimum*) is a hardy perennial that grows to 30 in.

Cilantro is always used fresh, because it is not suitable for drying. Being very susceptible to heat, the leaves should always be added to cooked dishes right at the end of cooking time, otherwise the flavor vanishes.

Quillquiña comes from Bolivia. It is reminiscent of cilantro and should be used in the same way.

Vietnamese coriander, or rau ram, smells like cilantro, but has a peppery, bitter taste.

Fitweed has a very strong cilantro taste. It is used to season the Thai hot-sour soup "ton yum".

Vap ca has a fresh, somewhat lemony aroma, similar to Vietnamese coriander. It is used to season soups and meat.

Sea arrowgrass is a northern European substitute for cilantro. It is particularly good in a pork and barley stew.

○ **Kitchen know-how**

More than any other herb, cilantro is typical of Latin American — especially Mexican — and Asian cuisines. The use of cilantro in Asia can be compared to that of parsley elsewhere, which earned it the alternative name of Chinese parsley. Coriander root is also very popular in Asia. It is used in combination with garlic, chili and cilantro, especially for marinades. **Quillquiña** (*Porphyllum ruderale*), also called killi, is an essential component of Bolivian salsa. Used in Bolivia as a herbal remedy as well as an everyday seasoning, it grows at altitudes of up to 8800 ft.

high in temperate and cold zones on salt meadows and along beaches. It forms upright, fleshy stems with narrow, linear, grassy, fleshy leaves, which are gathered before the little greenish flowers blossom. The relatively tough outer layer and the thin leaves mean that there is little evaporation, which enables the plant to grow in the salty conditions.

CALAMINT

In addition to the well-known mint plants of the genus *Mentha*, there are other varieties, such as **calamint** (*Calamintha sylvatica*, syn. *Calamintha officinalis*), that have a mint-like flavor. Calamint is a perennial plant that grows in light woods from central and southern Europe to the southwest Ukraine. Its low, creeping root produces upright, sprigged, square stems with slightly curved leaves. The flowers are violet to purple. It was cultivated as a salad vegetable in England in the Middle Ages. **Garden calamint** (*Calamintha grandiflora*) is a flat, aromatic plant with stemmed, broad oval, hairy leaves that bend under slightly, producing pink panicles. **Roman calamint** (*Calamintha* sp.) grows wild against walls and has pink flowers. **American calamint** (*Pycnanthemum pilosum*) is, as its names implies, a native of North America. The long, narrow, hairy leaves and the buds of the white flowers are used as seasoning.

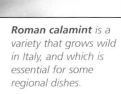

Roman calamint *is a variety that grows wild in Italy, and which is essential for some regional dishes.*

Calamint *is a delicate, slender plant with a strong scent of mint that is similar to that of camphor.*

American calamint *has a particularly strong minty flavor.*

Garden calamint *has a pleasant, aromatic minty flavor, which is particularly good in a herbal tea.*

○ **Kitchen know-how**

All varieties of mint have a strong aromatic to astringent or spicy taste. Varieties that contain menthol leave a refreshing, cool feeling in the mouth, which develops fully only in combination with sugar. When sweetened, the delicate nuances of the different varieties, such as pineapple, apple, ginger and orange mint, come to the fore. The same applies to the biting, acidic, menthol freshness of spearmint and peppermint, which develops fully in cold, refreshing drinks. For delicate desserts, such as gelatine desserts and custards, sherbets and granitas (pictured left), and for jams too, varieties with a more delicate flavor are more suitable. However, this does not mean that only desserts can be flavored with mint. Spearmint is used to make traditional mint sauce, while powerful peppermint is an essential ingredient in Indian mint chutney, which must be freshly prepared. In addition to the omnipresent mint tea, mint is an extremely popular seasoning for meat (especially lamb and goat) in the Arabian countries, usually combined with lots of garlic, as in minted lamb kebabs. In the national cuisine of Southeast Asia mint is used in meat dishes that contain a lot of chili, and in Vietnam it is used with cilantro to season the salads that are served with every meat and fish dish.

MINT

People have been mad about mint for centuries. The leaves of most mints contain a volatile oil with a high menthol content. Approximately twenty varieties of mint are spread across the temperate zones of Europe, the Near East, North Africa, and North America. A confusing plethora of mint varieties have grown up as a result of hybridizing and crossing. **Water mint** (*Mentha aquatica*), a parent of peppermint, can still be found growing wild in Europe. It is self-seeding, grows in damp spots, and prefers shade. The greenish-red leaves give off a delicate scent. Because of its very strong taste it is rarely used in cooking. **Horsemint** (*Mentha longifolia*) also grows wild in Europe. The plant has long, narrow, gray leaves and purple flowers. It is not used in cooking. **Field mint** (*Mentha arvensis*), sometimes called corn mint, can also be found growing wild. The flowers of field mint and water mint are different from those of other varieties of mint, being arranged in whorls in the crux of the leaves rather than at the end of the stem. The oval-shaped leaves of field mint, which are slightly pointed at the ends, are veined in dark red and slightly notched or saw-toothed. Several types of mint are descended from the **round-leafed mint** (*Mentha suaveolens*), of which the **apple mint** (*Mentha rotundifolia*) is of interest for culinary purposes. It has large, hairy green leaves. **Spearmint**

Catnip (*Nepeta cataria*) *has a magical effect on cats, and in France is also used to season salad dressings.*

Pineapple mint (Mentha suaveolens *var. variegata*) *has brilliant, green leaves variegated with yellow and a fruity flavor.*

Hairy curly mint *is one of the many cultivated varieties of curly mint.*

Smooth curly mint *does not taste noticeably different from the hairy variety. .*

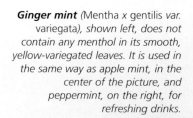

Ginger mint (Mentha x gentilis *var. variegata), shown left, does not contain any menthol in its smooth, yellow-variegated leaves. It is used in the same way as apple mint, in the center of the picture, and peppermint, on the right, for refreshing drinks.*

(*Mentha spicata*) is a lightly hairy type of mint with long leaves. Its oil is used not only in candy, but also in toiletries. It is often mistaken for **garden mint**, which is a cross between *Mentha suaveolens* and *Mentha longifolia*. The lack of hairs on the fresh green leaves is typical — only the veins on the undersides of the leaves bear a few hairs. There are various types of **curly mint**. Most cultivated varieties, such as Turkish mint (*Mentha spicata* var. *crispa*), are descended from the garden mint. The curly, bright green leaves are very decorative. The oldest known mint variety is **peppermint** (*Mentha* x *piperita*), which is a hybrid of water mint and garden mint. Peppermint is the most important cultivated form of mint. Oil for industrial use is produced from the stemmed, oval, hairy leaves by steam distillation. It is highly aromatic, and has a burning taste at first, then refreshing, and is used for essences, liqueurs, and candy. Bergamot mint (*Mentha* x *piperita* var. *citrata*), also called orange or lemon mint, is derived from peppermint, and can be identified by the lack of menthol and its reddish-green leaves. **Eau de Cologne mint**, which smells like the perfume of the same name, is a little bigger than orange mint and has smooth, aromatic, purple-edged dark green leaves on reddish stems. **European pennyroyal** (*Mentha pulegium*) is the only variety of mint that contains poisonous pulegone, and should thus be treated with care. It has bright green leaves and purplish flowers.

Austrian mint (Mentha x gentilis) *has dark green, smooth leaves, and a soft, slight perfumed aroma.*

Spearmint, *one of the most popular mints, is used to make mint sauce, which is served with lamb dishes.*

Moroccan mint (Mentha spicata var. crispa) *is a small plant with a sweet, cool taste. The leaves are used in mint tea.*

Bergamot mint *has reddish-green leaves, which do not contain menthol and have a fruity taste.*

Turkish mint (Mentha spicata var. crispa) *has very curly leaves and tastes similar to caraway.*

Silver mint (Mentha longifolia) *leaves are long, narrow, and covered in a thick down of filaments, and give off a fresh scent.*

The "Mitcham" variety *is one of the best known of all peppermints, and is used to make teas and desserts.*

Water mint *is rarely used in cooking because of its strong flavor.*

BALM AND HYSSOP

Lemon balm (*Melissa officinalis*), which originated in the Near East, is now cultivated in Europe, North Africa and America. It was greatly prized by the Greeks and Romans, as its nectar has a strong attraction for honeybees (Greek *melissa* = bee). From a perennial rootstock, the plant puts forth square stems in spring, which can grow to 3 ft high and which die back in winter. The young, oval, serrated leaves, which are covered with hairs on the upper side, are gathered before the flowering period and used in cooking fresh or dried, whole or chopped. In herbal medicine lemon balm is used to reduce cholesterol levels in the blood.

○ Kitchen know-how

Lemon balm provides freshness in cooking. The leaves, which should be as young as possible, are not usually used on their own. They blend well in mixes of herbs that are used cold and where a fresh, lemony flavor is required, especially in salad dressings. Lemon balm can also be used wherever lemon juice or lemon zest is required. The leaves should be roughly chopped, and should not be cooked. Whole leaves are popular as a garnish for desserts, fruit salads, punches, and liqueurs; they also look attractive when frozen in ice cubes and served in drinks. As the flavor evaporates when the leaves are steeped in hot water, large quantities have to be used to make tea. Lemon balm should always be used fresh. In the salad shown here the fresh taste complements tomatoes, cottage cheese, and olives.

*This variety of catnip (*Nepeta cataria ssp.* citriodora) is native to Germany, where it is called white lemon balm. It smells slightly of lemon and is used in tea.*

*Moldavian melissa (*Dracocephalum moldavica*) has a mild lemony taste that is suitable for tea.*

*Wild monarda (*Monarda fistulosa ssp.* menthifolia) is native to North America and is used in the same way as oregano.*

It is a stimulant, strengthens the nerves and stomach, relieves flatulence and sweating and increases bile secretion. **Monarda**(*Monarda didyma*), or bee balm, is native to North America, where for centuries the Oswego Indians have prepared an aromatic tea from the leaves (hence its other common name, Oswego tea). This was used by the colonists as a substitute for imported tea following the Boston Tea party in 1773, at the start of the War of Independence. Monarda is a highly aromatic plant. The square stem, which grows to 3 ft high from the root, produces oval to lanceolate, serrated leaves and red labiate flowers, which are used fresh or dried in the kitchen. There are various varieties, which differ in the color of flowers and aroma.

Lemon balm gives off a strong smell of lemon when touched.

Scarlet monarda smells like orange bergamot and faintly of lemon, and is used to make an aromatic infusion.

The aroma of purple monarda is similar to that of camphor. The plant is used in fruit salads and preserves.

compared to mint in taste. **Sawtooth mint** (*Agastache urticifolia*), or nettle-leaf giant hyssop, grows wild in Idaho. The delicate leaves and pale pink candle-shaped flowers are used to prepare a tea. **Anise hyssop** (*Agastache anisata*) grows up to 8 in. high and produces long candles of lilac-colored flowers. The oval to triangular leaves have a pointed tip and are deeply serrated. They were used by the Native Americans in the preparation of drinks and as a flavoring. **Giant Mexican hyssop** (*Agastache mexicana*) grows wild in Mexico and has magenta-pink single flowers. The leaves and stems are infused to make a drink that is used in herbal medicine as a nerve tonic. **Korean mint** (*Agastache rugosa*) comes from northern Asia. It is very similar in appearance to anise hyssop, but has a definite mint-like smell. In eastern Asia and the United States it is cultivated as a herbal medicine, a culinary herb, and a perfume.

Hyssop has a slightly bitter, refreshing and aromatic minty taste. It bears opposite leaves, and has attractive blue or pink flowers.

Hyssop (*Hyssopus officinalis*) is a perennial herb native to southern Europe, southern Russia, the Middle East, and North Africa. The narrow, lanceolate leaves, which are arranged in whorls around the square stems, are hairy and have numerous deeply embedded oil glands on both sides. Depending on the variety, hyssop produces white, pinkish, or royal-blue labiate flowers. The young leaves and shoots can be picked continuously. The herb is used both fresh and dried; for drying, foliage picked during the flowering season is best. Hyssop is similar in taste to thyme and sage, but should be used sparingly. The bitter constituents in the leaves aid the digestion of fatty foods. Hyssop is used as a cure for colds and to relieve sweating. **Agastache** plants are native to North America, and can be

○ Kitchen know-how

Hyssop is ideally suited to seasoning meat. The powerful flavor is reminiscent of a mixture of thyme and sage, and goes well with roast or broiled pork, veal, lamb, and poultry, but can be cooked with the meat for only a short time.

Korean mint *tastes and smells like mint. It is used to make a refreshing tea and to flavor drinks.*

Anise hyssop *gives off a scent similar to licorice and anise, and enhances sweet dishes and herb teas.*

Giant Mexican hyssop *leaves are used like tarragon, to flavor slightly sour foods.*

CRESS AND COMPANIONS

Scurvy grass, or spoonwort (*Cochlearia officinalis*), is a perennial, evergreen plant that grows on salty, damp ground in coastal regions in northern climates. Its spoon-like leaves can be picked all year round. Because of the high vitamin C content it was formerly used as a preventive against scurvy, hence its name. The plant is also effective as a stomach treatment and diuretic. **Garden cress** (*Lepidium sativum*) originated in Persia. Today it is the most important of approximately eighty varieties in the Lepidium family. It is cultivated specially in market gardens, and is harvested throughout the year. A few days after germination both clover-like leaves are cut off close to the ground. For this reason the long-stemmed base leaves and feathery-stemmed leaves, as well as the white to pink flowers, are virtually unknown to most consumers. **Watercress** (*Nasturtium officinale*) originated in southeast Europe and western Asia and was very popular by the time of the Greeks and Romans. Today it has spread throughout the world. It grows in clear springs, slow-running water, ponds, and damp ditches to an altitude of 8200 ft. A herbaceous, perennial water plant, it has a long root system. The dark green, fleshy leaves grow on long stems above the water, where they can be harvested early in spring, and again later in the year. Watercress should be picked only from completely clean water, and should be washed carefully, because insect larvae often make their home in it. The herb should be transported and kept in water so that the full flavor is retained. If watercress is to be kept for any length of time, it should be placed in cold water (taking care not to immerse the leaves) rather than being stored in the refrigerator. In herbal medicine watercress, which has a high vitamin and mineral content, is used to purify the blood and to reduce fevers. The delicate taste of **broad-leafed cress** (*Lepidium latifolium*) is similar to that of garden cress. Even the roots of this perennial plant, native to the European coast, taste typically of garden cress. **Winter cress** (*Barbarea vulgaris*) is a hardy wild plant, which grows up to 30 in. high and has smooth or slightly hairy leaves and yellow flowers. It grows on damp clay soil, river banks, and by the side of roads in southwest Europe, Asia, and North Africa. The long-stemmed leaves are tripinnate with an oval tip, and are picked in winter and spring before flowering. When dried, the high vitamin C content is lost. Winter cress can be confused with field mustard (*Sinapsis arvensis*), which has little taste and is unimportant for culinary purposes. **The nasturtium** (*Tropaeolum majus*),

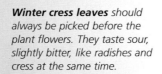

Winter cress leaves should always be picked before the plant flowers. They taste sour, slightly bitter, like radishes and cress at the same time.

Young nasturtium leaves go well in a mixed leaf salad. The leaves have a sour and peppery flavor. Simply snip them off the plant, wash, and add to the salad.

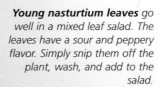

All parts of the nasturtium — the young leaves and the buds, the flowers and the fruit — taste sour and peppery. The wonderful flowers are an ideal garnish for many dishes.

sometimes called Indian cress, is an annual plant native to Peru, and is very susceptible to frost. The flat, shield or kidney-shaped leaves contain a glycoside, glucotropaeolin, which is responsible for the acidic taste. If preserved in vinegar and salt, the green unripe buds of the nasturtium can be used as a substitute for capers. The young leaves and flowers are supposed to purify the blood. If eaten in large quantities, they can irritate the stomach.

○ Kitchen know-how

From the point of view of taste, these plants can be divided into two groups. Garden cress and nasturtium have the typical cress taste, while watercress and winter cress have a sharper, more bitter, radish-like taste. They should all be used sparingly, so that the sharpness is refreshing and does not overwhelm other flavors. The leaves are usually eaten raw and add a pleasantly piquant note to salads. They also taste good in sandwiches, or as a garnish for soup, cream cheese, and potato dishes. The taste of cress also combines well with apples, oranges, mandarins, and lemons. Only the small, young or newly grown nasturtium leaves are good to eat; the bigger leaves are leathery and sour. The splendid blooms should be used with restraint. Like the leaves, the flowers have a strong peppery, sour taste and therefore are not suited to every dish. The finely chopped fruit provides a very spicy seasoning for roast pork or veal, for example, or for broiled fish.

The powerful, spicy, piquant and rather radish-like taste of garden cress is due to the glucotropaeolin and bitter components in the plant.

Watercress tastes dry and piquant, rather like radishes and mustard. The leaves should be picked before the plant flowers.

In Asia watercress is sold complete with the roots. The plant is cooked whole as a vegetable, while the leaves are used in salads.

Watercress found growing wild should be washed carefully before use.

Scurvy grass tastes slightly salty, with a sharp bite, rather like cress. If used sparingly, it is suitable for seasoning salads, sauces, and potato dishes. The leaves can also be boiled.

BAY AND MYRTLE

Bay (*Laurus nobilis*), sweet bay or sweet laurel, is an evergreen tree, a native of the Mediterranean, which still grows wild there today. In antiquity laurel wreaths were a symbol of victory and fame. In ancient Greece the plant was dedicated to Apollo, the sun god, who was depicted on coins crowned with a wreath of laurel leaves. At the Olympic Games sporting achievements were rewarded with a silver or gold-plated laurel wreath. Supposedly, the tradition of graduating from university with the degree of bachelor dates back to the custom in the Middle Ages of crowning academics and successful scholars with a crown of laurel leaves, a *bacca laurea*, which means bachelor in English. Bay is best known today for its culinary uses, especially as an appetite stimulant and a component of bouquet garni. The bay tree, which grows to 30 ft high, is cultivated commercially in the Mediterranean in huge plantations. In temperate latitudes it is grown only in tubs so that it can be easily protected in the cooler climate — it cannot withstand temperatures more than a few degrees below freezing. The leaves are olive green, sometimes rather brown, lanceolate, smooth-edged and leathery. The surface is shiny, the underside matt, with a sharply defined central spine and clearly visible veins. The fresh or dried leaves, with the stems removed, are used whole, crumbled or ground. The dried, whole leaves are the most valuable and have the

most intense flavor, which they lose after a year. Generally, bay should be used only in small doses. Because the flavor is imparted gradually, long cooking times are necessary to extract it fully. The leaves are then removed from the dish before serving. In the countries where bay is cultivated, oil produced from the berries is used to make liqueurs and as a medicinal rub. An infusion of bay leaves relieves stomach and kidney problems and promotes digestion. An important tip for anyone who wants to pick wild bay leaves is that *laurus nobilis* is the only member of the bay family that is not poisonous. This warning applies particularly to the **cherry laurel** (*Prunus laurocerasus*), whose leaves look like bay, but are darker and contain a poisonous bitter-almond-flavor oil. **Myrtle** (*Myrtus communis*) is an aromatic, evergreen plant, which grows to 16 ft in height in the Mediterranean mountains, North Africa, and central Europe. It grows as a potted plant in temperate climates. Myrtle was a symbol of love and eternal life in ancient times. The leaves are large, oval, shiny, dark green on top and pale green underneath. The stems are reddish; as the plant gets older they become woody and take on a grayish-beige color. The creamy-white flowers develop into purple-black berries, which, dried and ground, are used primarily as a spice in Greek cooking.. Tea can be made from the leaves, which can be picked all year round. Myrtle relieves flatulence and helps to relieve cold symptoms.

Stuffed sardines, sarde beccaficco. *This Sicilian recipe is a good example of powerful seasoning with bay leaves. Bay combines extremely well with sardines, garlic, and cheese.*

Bay *(on the left) and myrtle (on the right) are particularly good for powerful, hearty dishes.*

○ Kitchen know-how

Bay is a powerful seasoning with a spicy, dry, slightly bitter taste. It can be used to enhance all savory dishes. Dried bay leaves, which are included in a bouquet garni, are used to flavor meat dishes such as *osso bucco* and numerous game dishes, and will disguise the taste of mutton. Fresh bay leaves are used mainly in marinades, for preserving meat and herring, with mushrooms and in fish stocks.. Bay leaves are removed before a dish is served. **Myrtle**, which tastes of pepper, is used to stuff fish, together with fennel and thyme.

BASIL

Basil (*Ocimum basilicum*) is a native of India, but had spread to central Europe by the twelfth century and is today cultivated everywhere, both in the tropics and in temperate zones. This strongly scented plant is one of the most important culinary herbs. The plants are perennial in their native environment, but in cooler regions are usually annuals, because they are sensitive to cold (they cannot stand temperatures below 50°F for any length of time) and frost. The squarish stalks grow to 20 in. high and branch off strongly. The white labial flowers are arranged around the ends of the stems in whorls. The leaves are stemmed, longish, oval, and smooth or very slightly serrated. There are many different types of basil, with different growth patterns, sizes, shapes, textures, and colors of leaves. **Wild basil** (*Ocimum canum*) is very robust; it also grows in poor summers, and has slightly hairy leaves and pink flowers. **Lemon basil** (*Ocimum basilicum* var. *citriodorum*) is a delicate, compact variety with small leaves and white flowers. **Bush basil** (*Ocimum basilicum* var. *minimum*), also known as dwarf and Greek basil, grows to only 15 in. high and has small leaves. **Fever plant** (*Ocimum gratissimum*), also called tea bush or clover basil, is a warmth-loving plant native to east India. It has large, hairy, lime-green leaves and yellow flowers. **Camphor basil** (*Ocimum kilimandscharicum*) is a woody plant from Kenya, where it is cultivated commercially for its camphor content. **Sacred basil** (*Ocimum sanctum*), which has red and green varieties, also comes from India and is regarded as holy there and

○ Kitchen know-how

Basil, tomatoes, and garlic create an unbeatable taste combination and one that has innumerable variations, from tomato sauce with onions, garlic, and lots of fresh basil, to tomato and mozzarella salad with fresh basil. Fresh basil is the main ingredient in pesto, the classic Italian pasta sauce. Garlic, olive oil, pine nuts or peeled walnuts, salt, and strong Parmesan or pecorino cheese are added to basil in the standard recipe, but along the Ligurian coast, from Genoa to Provence (where this sauce is called pistou) there are many different versions. Basil is not just a "must" for tomato sauce and pesto; it is also a component of *herbes de Provence*. For most dishes that call for basil, cook only some of the herb and add the rest fresh just before serving.

Basil in plastic pots can be found in many supermarkets nowadays. Market gardening makes this possible. Just four weeks after the seeds are sown, the plants, which are extremely sensitive to cold, are wrapped in plastic and within a day are on their way in temperature-controlled trucks. Almost all varieties of basil make good houseplants because they like the warmth. Always pick a whole stalk and not just individual leaves, but always leave a few leaves on the plant so that it can continue to grow.

in Thailand, where it is grown next to Buddhist temples. Other varieties of basil, which have resulted from crossings and cultivation, are designated *Ocimum* species. For seasoning, fresh whole leaves, or rubbed or ground dried leaves are used. Basil is generally available in pots and grows well indoors in a sunny position. Because the fresh leaves are extraordinarily susceptible to bruising and discolor easily it is best to pick whole stems of leaves rather than individual ones; this also helps the plant to bush out. In cooking, basil should be added last to the recipe, to preserve its flavor. Basil can be preserved in oil: sprinkle each layer with salt, cover with olive oil, and close the container tightly. The basil will turn darker during storage (eventually it will turn black) but will not lose its flavor. Because basil reduces flatulence, it is a popular ingredient in dishes with pulses and cabbage; it also acts as a diuretic and promotes perspiration, and is a calmative. A pot of basil on your windowsill will keep flies away.

A farmer is selling fresh basil at a market in Aix-en-Provence. From Provence to Genoa basil is one of the most popular herbs. The peppery, spicy, rather sweet, refreshing taste of basil is at its very best when combined with tomatoes and garlic.

Green ruffles, or curly basil, has large, finely curled leaves, which are very attractive.

Purple ruffles has large, dark red leaves and deep pink flowers.

The fever plant has a strong scent, and the leaves make a very good tea.

Dark opal basil, another red-leafed form, has a scent more like that of carnations than basil.

Salad-leaf basil grows especially well. The smooth, tender leaves are preferred in Italy.

Anise basil is used in Persia, Thailand and Vietnam in sweet dishes.

Wild basil has a peppery flavor that goes well in hot dishes.

Green sacred basil has reddish-violet stems and veins. It is aromatic and spicy.

Red sacred basil has a very strong, sweet basil flavor. The leaves and flowers are ideal for sweet dishes and are very important in spicy Thai specialities.

Green bush basil has a strong flavor and is often grown for decoration.

Red bush basil, shown here in flower, is a compact, red leafed variety.

Thai basil looks like anise basil, but its flowers are red rather than purple.

Lemon basil has a fresh, lemony scent and is ideal in a green or tomato salad.

Fino verde has very slightly serated leaves, and is often used in pesto.

Neapolitan basil is one of the best for flavor. The leaves can grow quite large.

Mexican spice, or cinnamon, basil has red stems, pink leaves, and a sweet, intense flavor.

Camphor basil has a strong camphor scent, but can be used in mixed herbs.

Baby basil, or Greek dwarf basil, is usually grown in a pot.

The taste of wild oregano native to other countries may be quite different from that of the oregano from Sicily.

The best-flavored oregano is harvested in limestone areas around the Mediterranean, in June, when it is in full bloom.

OREGANO AND MARJORAM

Oregano (*Origanum vulgare*) is a native of the Mediterranean area and Asia, where it still grows wild in all dry, warm locations. It has been spread throughout the world and is cultivated mainly in Spain, Italy, and the United States. The plant, which grows up to 3 ft in height, forms squarish, reddish-brown stems, which bear broad, oval leaves. The leaves are collected while the plant is in bloom and are used fresh or dried, rubbed or ground, in cooking. The lower, thicker parts of the stem are of no value. The spicy, piquant, aromatic, dryish-bitter taste is reminiscent of marjoram and thyme, but oregano is much more acidic. Oregano is very well suited to drying and retains its flavor for up to a year if it is kept in an airtight container away from the light. As a medicinal plant it has an antispasmodic effect, is a decongestant, and prevents inflammation. **Small-leaf oregano** (*Origanum microphyllum*) is a native of Crete. **Winter marjoram** (*Origanum heracleoticum*) is a hardy plant that grows to 10 in. high and has small, white flowers. **Mexican**

Small-leaf oregano is an attractive, delicate variety with a mild, refreshing flavor.

Winter marjoram is also known as rigani. Its more sour, strong taste is similar to that of thyme.

Mexican oregano is very aromatic in dishes made with chili and meat.

dried. Dried marjoram is rubbed for use in cooking, as ground marjoram has only a very faint flavor. Good quality fresh marjoram can be identified by the powerful smell when the leaves are rubbed between two fingers — it smells better fresh than dried — and should feel hard. If marjoram is cooked at temperatures in excess of 175°F, its flavor becomes weaker, due to the formation of sulfurous compounds. Fresh marjoram prevents fatty foods from turning rancid quickly, while old marjoram speeds up the process. Marjoram promotes digestion and stimulates the appetite. **Crete marjoram** (*Origanum dictamnus*), sometimes also called dittany-of-Crete, has pendulous pink flowers and silvery leaves, which are used in herbal medicine to stop bleeding.

Marjoram *is picked before the big flower buds open, because the plant has the best flavor at this time.*

Marjoram *is commonly used, fresh or dried, in combination with onions and garlic.*

oregano (*Lippia graveolens*) is a North American variety of oregano and is often used in seasoning mixes for chili con carne. **Marjoram** (*Origanum majorana*) is a perennial plant that originated in the eastern Mediterranean and still grows wild in many forms. It is frequently cultivated as an annual in the colder regions of the northern hemisphere. On squarish stems, which grow to 20 in. high, marjoram bears small, oval, smooth-edged, silky-haired leaves. These are gathered when the flower buds are formed and are used fresh or

○ Kitchen know-how

Oregano seems to be associated with typical Italian seasoning, although, in actuality, this herb is used in relatively few dishes in Italy; the fact that it is used in pizza explains why it is so well known. In addition to enhancing the taste of pizza, oregano is an excellent seasoning for roast or broiled veal and pork. Although oregano is often used on its own because of its strong flavor, in southern Italy it is also often combined with basil and capers in tomato dishes. **Marjoram** is the perfect herb for fatty meat and is therefore especially popular in countries with hearty national dishes. Many different pork dishes can be seasoned with a combination of marjoram, onions, and garlic. Marjoram also goes exceptionally well with most combinations of vegetables and meat, especially in casseroles with pulses and smoked meat, where it can be combined successfully with peppery savory.

Dittany *(Cunila origanoides), or stonemint, has leaves that taste like oregano.*

Marjoram *has the best flavor when fresh. It is aromatic, spicy, a little bitter and similar to camphor.*

Crete marjoram *tastes milder than winter marjoram. It can be used to make a tangy tea.*

PARSLEY AND CELERY

Parsley (*Petroselinum crispum*) is native to the eastern Mediterranean but now is found throughout the world, and has, to some extent, gone back to its wild state. The biennial plant has long turnip-like roots, which cannot be used in cooking and should not be confused with the edible turnip-rooted, or Hamburg, parsley (*Petroselinum crispum* var. *tuberosum*). The stem grows to 4 ft high. The leaves are smooth at first, double or triple pinnate and with irregular serrations. There are also cultivated curly leafed varieties. The greenish-yellow umbels contain caraway-like seeds. The leaves are used fresh as a seasoning; the flavor is not as strong when dried. Parsley contains high levels of provitamin A, vitamins C and E, as well as iron and calcium. Parsley is a diuretic. Dog poison, or poisonous fool's parsley (*Aethusa cynapium*), can easily be mistaken for flat-leafed parsley. **Japanese parsley** (*Cryptotaenia japonica*), or mitsuba, is a perennial plant native to

Japan, Korea, and China. The tri-lobed leaves grow on thin, white stems up to 7 in. long. Depending on the variety, they can be pale or dark green. In Japan the leaves or leaf stems are used fresh, but more usually they are blanched. Japanese parsley goes well with bitter vegetables and salads, and is used as a garnish for sashimi, a raw fish dish. **Wild celery** (*Apium graveolens* var. *secalinum*) is a biennial plant found in many parts of the world. The aromatic, curly or flat leaves are used whenever a celery taste is wanted, often as a flavoring in soup.

The flat-leafed variety of parsley is somewhat finer and has a more aromatic and spicier taste than that of curly parsley. However, curly parsley is milder and for this reason is popular for use as a garnish.

The leaves of wild celery are similar to those of flat-leafed parsley. They taste more strongly of celery, however, and, in contrast to parsley, are well-suited for drying.

Japanese parsley tastes similar to sorrel and celery. In Japan it is used chopped in soups and whole in tempura. When cooked, it develops a bitter taste.

○ Kitchen know-how

Parsley is the best known and most commonly used herb everywhere except Asia. Finely chopped parsley is used to season almost all types of food — soups, salads, sauces, potatoes, vegetables, and meat and fish dishes. It is indispensible to bouquet garni and *fines herbes*. Persillade (seen left) is a classic French herb mixture of finely chopped parsley, garlic, and shallots, which has gained international recognition as an accompaniment to sautéed meat and vegetables. It should be heated gently in order to retain the fresh flavor.

Aka-shiso, known as green cumin, has leaves with a slight peppery flavor. In Japan they are used with raw fish dishes.

PERILLA AND STINGING NETTLE

Perilla (*Perilla frutescens*), also known as shiso, is an annual, aromatic plant native to Burma, China, and Japan, where it has been cultivated for centuries as a spice, an oil-producing plant, a medicinal herb, and for its perfume and decorative properties. The square stems grow to 6 ft high and bear big, curved leaves and white and pink flowers. The whole plant is slightly hairy. All parts of the plant are used. Oil gathered from the seeds is used to flavor fish and tempura batter, as well as for the production of dyes, paints, and oil paper. Both green and red varieties are a traditional seasoning for sushi. **Stinging nettle** (*Urtica dioica*) grows in all the temperate regions of the world and is regarded as a weed, but can also be used as a culinary herb. The square stems, which grow to 3 ft high, have longish, oval leaves and catkins of tiny flowers. The whole plant is covered in hairs, which break off when touched and embed themselves in the skin like tiny needles, causing an unpleasant burning and itching sensation. For culinary purposes the young leaves are prepared in the same way as spinach. Old leaves, which contain many vitamins and minerals, should not be used because of the high proportion of tannin. Stinging nettle is a diuretic.

Ao-shiso, or red shiso, is used to color preserved fruit and vegetables. Preserved in vinegar, it is considered a delicacy in macrobiotic cooking.

Stinging nettle leaves lose their unpleasant sting when wilted or infused in hot water. They can be used in combination with other herbs in soups and salads.

Salad burnet is a perennial rosette-shaped plant suitable for every garden. The leaves are picked for use as an herb before the plant flowers.

Salad burnet could almost have been made for herb mixes. The original, mild flavor is very adaptable. It can be used liberally in fresh salad herb mixtures as well as in sauces. The flavor develops best in combination with vinegar and lemon juice.

○ Kitchen know-how

With its pleasantly refreshing, nutty, and cucumber-like flavor, salad burnet lends a refined note to many salads, herb mixes, and cream-cheese recipes. Because of its delicate flavor it should never be cooked, but added afterwards. The flavor also dissipates if the leaves are dried. Together with borage flowers, the leaves are used as a garnish for summery recipes and cooling drinks. **Burnet saxifrage** goes well with salads, herb sauces, vegetable soups, and egg and fish dishes. It is also used to flavor herb vinegars, cold drinks, and liqueurs.

SALAD BURNET, GREAT BURNET, AND SAXIFRAGE

Salad burnet (*Sanguisorba minor*), or burnet, is a native of Eurasia and is commonly found in meadows and dried grasses. The perennial, rosette-shaped plant has feathery, long-stemmed base leaves. The pinnate leaves are oval to round in shape and heavily serrated. The leaves, which are picked before the plant flowers, are used as an herb. They are particularly high in vitamin C. **Great burnet** (*Sanguisorba officinalis*) is a hardy plant that grows to $6^1/_2$ ft in height on damp meadows. The furrowed stems have azygous, pinnate, finely toothed leaves that look almost like filigree. The stems are used in herbal medicine as a styptic (a substance to stop the flow of blood). **Burnet saxifrage** (*Pimpenella saxifraga*), which grows to 20 in. in height, is a native of Europe that has spread elsewhere. More than 200 different varieties are known, with both wild and cultivated varieties being widespread. It has azygous, pinnate, delicate leaves, which form a rosette on the ground. The leaves and the root, which tastes of anise, are used as a seasoning. As a medicinal plant it is used for catarrh, whooping cough, stomachache and headache, and is also an effective cardiotonic.

Great burnet leaves are less flavorsome than those of the salad burnet, but can be used in cooking in the same way. They have a slightly sharp, cucumber taste. The plant is more important in herbal medicine, where the stems in particular are used.

Burnet saxifrage is very popular in French and Italian cooking. Young leaves should be used fresh; older leaves can be dried or frozen. They have an original, astringent flavor like that of borage and cucumber, and are best used in green salads.

Comfrey leaves are used fresh or dried. If the leaves are to be used as an herb, they must be picked before the plant flowers. Cutting back the pink flowers on the branching, roughly haired stems will produce a mass of leaves.

COMFREY AND GARDEN PURSLANE

Comfrey (*Symphytum officinale*) is native to Europe and Asia, and also common in North America. It grows to 32 in. high on damp soil. The lanceolate, slightly sweet leaves are used fresh or dried as a culinary herb. As the plant gets older the leaves become more bitter. European country wines are flavored with dried comfrey root, which smells rather like camphor.

Like all members of the *Symphytum* genus, comfrey contains high levels of minerals, protein, and vitamin B, and allantoin in the roots, which helps to form cells. Comfrey is a known herbal remedy for breathing disorders and is often made into a tea to aid digestion. It is used externally for broken bones, bruises, swelling, and burns. **Garden purslane** (*Portulaca oleracea* ssp. *sativa*) is an annual that grows to 12 in. high and flourishes in temperate and warm zones on every continent. It is descended from the wild form, which is native to Eurasia and is cultivated in many countries. It bears oval to spade-shaped leaves on the smooth, very fleshy, slightly reddish stem. For culinary use the leaves, which taste acidic, salty, and faintly aromatic, and have a fairly high vitamin C content, are harvested before the plant flowers. Because the herb tastes salty, there is no need to add further salt to the food. Young seedlings can be eaten like cress. In folk medicine purslane is used for purifying the blood and to increase production of gastric juices. Purslane was formerly used as a cooling herb: the refreshing leaves relieve thirst.

Garden purslane *is sold in large quantities in Mexican markets. It is used as a salad herb in regional cuisine, but can also be used as a vegetable, similar to spinach.*

Comfrey Bocking No.4

Garden purslane leaves *should be as fresh as possible when used. They are a suitable accompaniment to salads, soups, sauces, cream cheese, and raw fruit and vegetables. In the Far East garden purslane is eaten as a vegetable. For a long time the buds were used as a substitute for capers.*

LOVAGE AND ROSEMARY

Lovage (*Levisticum officinale*), a native of Iran, Afghanistan, and southern Europe that is cultivated in many countries, takes several years to grow to its full height of 8 ft. Every year it forms a many-headed bulb, which produces a rosette of double or triple pinnate leaves with wide wedge-shaped incisions. The leaves are smooth, shiny green, and rather leathery. In summer upright, thick, hollow stems grow with double umbels of pale yellow flowers at the tips. Every part of the plant contains flavorings and can be used in cooking: fresh and dried, rubbed and ground leaves; dried and ground roots and seeds. Dried leaves lose their flavor after about six months, but fresh leaves are suitable for freezing. Lovage is one of the herbs that can be added to food while it is cooking. When rubbed, the fresh leaves give off a scent reminiscent of the well-known seasoning Maggi. However, despite the similarity in aroma and the fact that it is a herbal extract, Maggi does not contain lovage. The flavor of lovage root is even stronger than that of the leaves. When cooked, the roots and stems can have an overwhelming taste. The dried seeds are used to flavor bread and pastries, and should be used sparingly. A sprig of tarragon and lovage can be used to flavor a bottle of vinegar. As lovage is quickly and easily overcome by insects, the herb should be stored away from light. Tea can be prepared from lovage for use as a diuretic and as an aid for stomach and digestive complaints. **Scottish lovage** (*Ligusticum scoticum*), or sea parsley, grows on the northern Atlantic coasts. Its roots are used in medicine as a mild sedative.

Rosemary can be either fresh or dried. Oil flavored with rosemary can be served with any fresh green salad. The flavor of rosemary goes best, however, with rabbit. To make the rabbit legs with rosemary shown here, washed legs are seasoned with salt, pepper, and garlic, and covered with sprigs of rosemary, then wrapped in strips of bacon, sealed and browned in hot oil, dotted with butter and baked for 20 minutes in an oven preheated to 425°F..

Lovage should be used carefully, because the penetrating flavor can easily become overpowering. This also applies to mixes of herbs that contain lovage.

Scottish lovage has a powerful, spicy taste, and less of the penetrating yeast-like flavor of common lovage.

○ Kitchen know-how

Rosemary, with its camphor-like, dry, bitter taste, goes well with all white meats and with Mediterranean vegetables, such as tomatoes and eggplants. In Italian cuisine rosemary is also used to flavor tomato soup, roast mutton and pork, cheese, and savory sauces. The unmistakable flavor of *pasta e fagioli* is also due to rosemary. Rosemary demonstrates its Mediterranean flair best when combined with wine and garlic. It is also popular for use in marinades and in game and fish dishes. **Lovage** is an everyday herb, so to speak, because it goes especially well with simple food. It is good in rustic stews, and with braised meat as well as in soups based on pulses with smoked bacon added. Its familiar flavor should not prevent its use in stylish cuisine, but it should be used with restraint.

***Fresh rosemary** is mass-produced outdoors as potted plants for sale in garden centers and supermarkets.*

Rosemary (*Rosmarinus officinalis*) is native to the Mediterranean region, where it grows wild, and is widespread throughout Europe and America. The aromatic, evergreen plant, which grows to 6½ ft in height, puts out shoots that turn woody in time. These bear rolled-up, leathery, smooth-edged leaves — smooth and green on top, hairy and whitish-gray underneath, and dotted with glands — that look like pine needles. The leaves are harvested during and after flowering and are used fresh or dried, whole, chopped, or ground. Fresh rosemary can easily be finely chopped and added to numerous recipes. The flavor is retained best if whole sprigs of rosemary are dried. Because of its strong taste, rosemary is used sparingly and is cooked with food to extract the maximum flavor. Large sprigs can be tied to meat or pushed into poultry to be roasted in the oven, and removed before serving. It lends an incomparable flavor to oil; one or two fresh sprigs will suffice for 2¼ cups of oil. Rosemary burned on a barbecue or an open fire gives off an aromatic fragrance. The herb is very popular in France and Italy, and French rosemary is very highly rated. An antioxidant, rosemary extends the life of foodstuffs. In herbal medicine it is used to stimulate the circulation and is recommended for use in the bath to calm the nervous system.

***Rosemary**, like thyme and lavender, grows wild in the Mediterranean scrubland and develops a particularly strong flavor in these arid areas. If you used the dried needles from rosemary grown there, you would need only half the usual quantity. Rosemary leaves and flowers can be picked all year round.*

***Cultivated rosemary**, as shown here, has a penetrating flavor. The many different varieties that are cultivated — upright, bushy, creeping — have different flavors; fresh and lemony (ARP, Salem), resinous (Gorizia), dry and camphor-flavored (Rex), or delicate, with a gentle flavor, like "Miss Yessop's Upright", one of the finest varieties.*

○ Kitchen know-how

Savory is an excellent seasoning for any dish that includes beans, in particular green beans, but it also brings out the flavor of many others, including peas, lentils, and casseroles based on pulses. The fresh, peppery, acidic flavor is also remarkable with stewed lamb. For poultry or game stock, two or three sprigs can be included in a bouquet garni, making the use of pepper unnecessary. Fresh or dried rubbed leaves also enhance the flavor of big, fatty pork or mutton roasts, as well as fish that are baked whole, such as carp, eel, and mackerel. The fresh, young leaves are used with tender meat such as veal and poultry, with baked fish, and fish steamed *en papillote*. A *court bouillon* for cooking crab and lobster also benefits from fresh savory. For raw vegetables and salads, only very fresh, very finely chopped leaves should be used, otherwise the peppery taste becomes unpleasant. It is best stirred into vinaigrettes.

Savory is particularly popular in many bean dishes, but the spicy flavor also goes well with many other foods. When dried, it retains its full flavor.

Savory is very aromatic. The taste is reminiscent of both oregano and thyme. The leaves are pleasantly soft and velvety.

SAVORY

Summer savory (*Satureja hortensis*). is an unassuming, annual plant native to the Black Sea and eastern Mediterranean areas. It is now cultivated in Europe and North America. The plant, which grows up to 31 in. high, forms a lightly branched bush. The lower branches are woody and the upper branches bear narrow, pointed leaves, which are dark green on top and gray or silvery underneath. **Winter savory** (*Satureja montana*) is a small, perennial, aromatic plant that is more robust than summer savory. Both are popular in cooking. Fresh green leaves can be taken from the plant at any time, but the flavor is at its fullest just before and during flowering. Savory is best if tied in bundles and hung up in a shaded, well-ventilated place to dry. Dried savory, whether rubbed, chopped, or ground, retains almost all of its original flavor. Savory is included in the French mixture *fines herbes*. It helps to curb flatulence and diarrhea, calm the nerves, strengthen the stomach, stimulate the appetite and is also very effective against bacteria.

Winter savory has a more powerful flavor than summer savory. The leaves are firm, almost hard, and rather tough, and therefore should be removed from a dish before it is served.

SWEET CICELY, MARIGOLD, AND REFLEX STONECROP

Sweet cicely (*Myrrhis odorata*), or garden myrrh, is a perennial plant that comes from central and northern Europe. The grooved, hollow stems, which grow to 3 ft high, bear large light-green leaves that are lightly hairy underneath and feather-shaped. They are used fresh in salads and for sweet dishes, but lose a lot of their flavor when dried. **Mexican marigold** (*Tagetes minuta*) is an annual, aromatic plant native to South America. On the smooth, upright stems, which grow to 10 ft in height, there are three to seven pinnate leaves. The leaves have a spicy lemon smell and in Mexico are used primarily in soups. The roots are effective against nematodes in the soil. **Tangerine marigold** (*Tagetes tenuifolia*) comes from Mexico and Central America, and has glowing orange flowers. The delicate, feathered leaves smell strongly of tangerines, and can

Sweet cicely *tastes sweetish and slightly aniseed. The flavor improves the acidic taste of fruit, and can be added to sweet dishes as a sugar substitute.*

The fresh, tender shoots of reflex stonecrop, *chopped or pounded in a pestle and mortar, make a good, slightly acidic seasoning for sauces and salads.* **Do not confuse it with the posionous biting stonecrop.**

be used to season sweet dishes, salads, and fruit punches. **Reflex stonecrop** (*Sedum rupestre*) is an evergreen, fleshy plant, native to Europe, where it grows on rocks and walls. It bears fleshy, cylindrical leaves and tiny, yellow star-shaped flowers on the low-lying shoots. Used as a salad herb, it must be carefully distinguished from the poisonous **biting stonecrop** (*Sedum acre*), also called wall-pepper.

Tagetes minuta

Tagetes tenuifolia

Plants from the genus Tagetes *can be identified by a fresh scent of citrus fruits.*

Yellow gentian *(*Gentiana lutea*) is cultivated for its roots, which are used as a bitter additive in alcoholic beverages.*

Turkish arugula has a pleasantly sharp, radish-like taste.

○ Kitchen know-how

These salad herbs are wild, although many of them are also cultivated nowadays. They lend a particular flavor to mixed salads or make their mark on their own, **sorrel** being the best example of this. The powerful acidic taste makes a refined spring salad when mixed with plenty of cooked onions and a touch of garlic, or in a delicate vinaigrette made from sherry vinegar and olive oil. All types of sorrel combine well with young, blanched **dandelion leaves** when dressed with walnut oil and raspberry vinegar. **Arugula** also goes well in a rustic salad of wild herbs but is not suitable for use on its own because of the strong taste. The flowers from wild herbs, available in profusion in spring, can be used as a garnish.

SALAD HERBS

There are some herbs that are not easy to classify, because they are neither true herbs nor green vegetables. Some can be used in generous quantities, either on their own or mixed with others, and are thus more like salad leaves than herbs, while others are used more sparingly. **Turkish arugula** (*Bunias orientalis*) is a strong perennial plant known in Poland, Turkey, and parts of Russia. **Arugula** (*Eruca vesicaria* ssp. *sativa*), also known as rocket or roquette, is a strongly scented annual plant, growing to 3 ft in height, which is native to the Mediterranean area and eastern Asia. **Rhubarb** (*Rheum rhabarbarum*) leaves make an interesting salad leaf, although usually only the long, fleshy stems are used. **Sorrel** (*Rumex acetosa*), native to central and western Europe, has ground-hugging, broad lanceolate leaves that can be prepared in the same way as spinach. Only fresh, young leaves are used, and they should not be cooked for long. If eaten in quantity, the oxalic acid they contain can cause kidney damage. **French sorrel** (*Rumex scutatus*) is a smooth-leafed plant, which can be distinguished from sorrel by its shield-shaped, succulent leaves. It also contains oxalic acid and should be eaten only in small quantitites. **Rue** (*Ruta graveolens*), or herb of grace, is native to the Mediterranean area, but today can be found growing wild in northern Europe, and is cultivated in both Europe and the United States. It has gray-green to bluish-green pinnate leaves, which are gathered for use before the plant flowers. Rue is used only in small quantities — and *never* by pregnant women — as in large amounts the leaves are poisonous. Touching the sap or even the leaves can result in an

Its refreshing, sharp, mustardy taste has made arugula an increasingly popular salad herb.

The lemony flavor of sorrel is very popular for use in salads and soups.

Wild sorrel is used in the same way as the cultivated plant. The delicate taste is slightly bitter and acidic.

French sorrel leaves and shoots have an intense citric acid flavor, but are less bitter than sorrel leaves.

Bistort does not have much taste as a salad ingredient, but can be used like spinach.

Rhubarb leaves have a high oxalic acid content, which can be reduced by adding sugar.

A salad of wild herbs cannot be made to order. You have to use what is in season, and all these herbs are really good only when they are young and tender. The composition should be balanced, with roughly equal quantities of bitter, acidic and garlic-flavored herbs (such as bear's garlic) for a perfect combination.

unpleasant skin inflammation. In Italy common rue is used in the manufacture of the grape spirit *grappa*, and in the past was also used in wine production. **Yellow sweet clover** (*Melilotus officinalis*), or yellow melilot, is an annual plant, which smells of coumarin and grows wild by the side of roads and in fields. **Wood sorrel** (*Oxalis acetosella*), or shamrock, is a wild plant with a high oxalic acid content, and therefore should be used only in very small quantities. The leaves are heart-shaped and sensitive to light. In homeopathy it is used to treat liver and digestive complaints. **Lucky clover** (*Oxalis deppei*), or good luck clover, originated in Mexico and was planted as vegetable in Europe in the eighteenth century. **Bennet** (*Geum urbanum*) is a perennial, hairy, semi-roseate plant that grows on damp sites. It is a popular wild vegetable, which combines well with stinging nettle and plantain. **Bistort** (*Polygonum bistorta*), also known as snakeweed and red legs, is a perennial plant that grows to 3 ft high. The stems and spear-shaped leaves can be prepared as a vegetable. **Cinquefoil** (*Potentilla anserina*), or silverweed, which grows on calcium-rich soil, puts out creeping runners from the roots and has yellow flowers shaped like chickens' feet. **Ground ivy** (*Glechoma hederacea*) is a creeping plant also known as field balm. **Dandelion** (*Taraxacum officinale*) is a very familiar rosette-shaped plant with toothed leaves and a single yellow flower. The plant contains insulin and a number of vitamins and minerals.

Yellow sweet clover has an unobtrusive fresh taste. A tea made from its leaves acts as a decongestant.

Wood sorrel can be used instead of sorrel to lend an acidic flavor to soups and sauces.

Bennet is slightly bitter. The young leaves are suitable for salads, and when boiled in salted water, as a vegetable.

The leaves and the turnip-shaped roots of lucky clover.can be boiled and eaten.

Cinquefoil has a refreshing, bitter taste. However, it is used only in small amounts in salads.

Rue has a spicy, sharp, slightly bitter taste. It can be used very sparingly in egg dishes and with cheese and game.

Ground ivy has a bitter, slightly sharp and dry taste. It gives off a mint-like scent.

The bitter taste of dandelion is perfect in salads with a dressing of walnut oil and red wine vinegar.

○ Kitchen know-how

Sage is a typical Mediterranean herb, and especially typical of Italian cuisine. In central Italy fresh sage leaves are tossed in butter, which is then used to prepare the sauces for many pasta dishes. Sage is excellent with meat, especially as a seasoning for fatty meat such as mutton, lamb, pork, and goose, where it is used for its ability to aid digestion. *Saltimbocca alla romana* is a well-known Roman speciality, which, as the name implies, leaps into the mouth as soon as it is served. This simple and refined combination of veal and ham sautéed in butter is unmistakably connected with the flavor of sage. Because sage has a very strong flavor, you need only one leaf per slice of meat. In Germany, sage is used to season eel. Mixed with diced onion, the leaves make a good stuffing for poultry. Fresh leaves are more perfumed and taste nicer than dried ones, which have an almost resinous, medicinal taste. The full flavor of sage develops best if it is cooked with food.

Sage *comes from the Mediterranean. The ancient Romans prized its healing properties as an astringent and disinfectant herb. Its botanical name,* Salvia, *comes from the Latin* salvare, *to heal.*

Greek sage *tastes bitter, its spicy, fresh flavor somewhere between that of ordinary sage and clary sage. In Greece it is dried and infused to make a tea.*

Clary sage *has a slightly bitter but typically sage taste. It can be used with eggs, in sweet dishes, and infused in a tea, and is used to flavor vermouth.*

The woody old sage roots *produce the best leaves with the strongest flavor. Sage can be harvested practically throughout the whole year; it even survives under a blanket of snow.*

SAGE

Sage (*Salvia officinalis*), a widely cultivated evergreen plant native to the Mediterranean region, grows up to 31 in. high. The felty, heavily haired leaves of the many varieties of sage are used fresh or dried, whole, chopped or ground, as a culinary herb. They are picked shortly before the plant flowers and have a powerful, spicy, aromatic flavor that is also bitter, slightly burning and astringent, reminiscent of camphor. The flavor varies considerably depending on the variety and location. Sage acts as a bacteriocide and is useful in counteracting stomach and intestinal inflammation. It is used as a gargle and in lozenges for sore throats, and prevents perspiration. **Greek sage** (*Salvia triloba*) puts forth velvety leaves that are felty-gray underneath, and has attractive, deep blue flowers. **Clary sage** (*Salvia sclarea*) grows wild in German vineyards, where the very large leaves were used to flavor wine and as a substitute for hops in making beer. **Purple sage** (*Salvia officinalis* var. *purpurascens*) is a small plant with striking purple leaves and bright blue flowers. **Dalmatian sage** (*Salvia officinalis* ssp. *major*) is a large-leafed variety native to the stark limestone cliffs of Dalmatia. This woody plant produces round leaves. **Tricolor sage** (*Salvia officinalis* var. *tricolor*) is a popular decorative plant, with green leaves that have a cream-colored border streaked with red. It has a mild flavor and is used less for cooking than for decoration. **Pineapple sage** (*Salvia rutilans*, syn. *Salvia elegans*) is a Mexican plant and is susceptible to frost. It produces carmine red flowers in autumn and smells of pineapple.

Meadow sage (*Salvia pratensis*) is not important either for cooking or medicine, because it contains only traces of essential oils.

Dalmatian sage has a sweetish, delicate sage flavor and a pleasantly mild, fresh aroma. It is the gourmet sage.

Fruit sage (Salvia dorisiana), not illustrated, is a sweet sage from Honduras and is reminiscent of guava in taste. The plant has heart-shaped, big, lime-green, hairy leaves, which are popular for use in sweet dishes or infused in a tea.

Tricolor, the attractive, colorful sage, has a slightly bitter, yet mild taste. It can also be used to season fatty meats and fish.

Pineapple sage smells seductively of pineapple, but the taste does not live up to the promise of the perfume. It is a pleasant flavoring for fish and salads.

Purple sage has a very intense taste. The slightly furred leaves can be used in the same way as normal sage. The flavor comes out especially well when infused in tea.

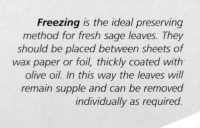

Freezing is the ideal preserving method for fresh sage leaves. They should be placed between sheets of wax paper or foil, thickly coated with olive oil. In this way the leaves will remain supple and can be removed individually as required.

Thyme from Haute Provence bears little resemblance to wild thyme. It has a more powerful flavor, which develops only under the southern sun. It combines especially well with typical local produce, such as that used in ratatouille.

Garden thyme has a spicy, sharp taste. When fresh, its strong aroma is more intense in summer than at other times of year. Commerciall,y it is usually available dried.

Lemon thyme has a strong lemony flavor, which goes with fish, eggs, and creamy sauces, and is outstanding combined with lamb.

○ Kitchen know-how

Thyme is one of the typical Mediterranean herbs and its taste has left its mark on the regional cuisine. The spicy taste combines ideally with garlic, olives, eggplant, tomatoes, peppers and zucchini. Its ability to aid digestion makes it an ideal herb for heavy and fatty food. Braising steak, game, lamb, dark poultry, meat, boiling sausages, and eel, as well as pulses and potatoes, all benefit from its spicy taste. Thyme is a permanent ingredient of the well-known herb mixtures *fines herbes*, bouquet garni and *herbes de Provence*. The powerful taste develops best at high temperatures. Thyme is added to food during the cooking process; and whole sprigs are removed before serving. When adding thyme, bear in mind that dried thyme is three times stronger than fresh. Together with tarragon and balm, it is used to produce herb vinegar. It lends a pleasant taste to pickles. Wild thyme is used in the same way as cultivated thyme.

THYME

There are various types of thyme, which differ in appearance and taste. **Garden thyme** (*Thymus vulgaris*) is a perennial plant native to southern Europe. It is cultivated throughout Europe and North America. The plant, which grows to 16 in. high, has small elliptical leaves that curl at the edges on partly woody stems. The leaves are felty and hairy underneath, and grayish-green in color. The pink to deep lilac flowers grow in heads at the end of stems. In cooking, thyme is used fresh, dried or frozen, roughly chopped, rubbed or ground. The leaves are picked just before the plant flowers, when they are at their most flavorsome. Thyme dries well, preferably in whole sprigs; the dried leaves are then stripped from the stalks. In herbal medicine thyme is used as an antispasmodic and decongestant. It is also administered in the form of a gargle for inflammations of the throat, and as cough medicine. Wild thyme (*Thymus serpyllum*) appears in many forms and varieties. The small, perennial, creeping plant flourishes in Europe, India, Iceland, the former Soviet Union, and America. It can form a large carpet. The leaves are a reverse egg shape and have clearly recognizable veins. Wild thyme is known to help strengthen the stomach. **Lemon thyme** (*Thymus x citriodorus*) is a cross between garden thyme and wild thyme. There are many cultivated forms of lemon thyme, which are either creeping plants or upright.

The flowers are colored from pale pink to violet. Many varieties of both thyme and lemon thyme are known as silver thyme. **Caraway thyme** (*Thymus herba-barona*) is a low-growing, creeping, variety of thyme that is a popular pot plant in Sardinia and Corsica. The flowers are pink and the leaves dark green. It is traditionally used as a seasoning for baron of beef. **Indian borage** (*Coleus amboinicus*), also called Jamaican thyme, grows wild in tropical Africa, in Namibia, and in Brazil. It is cultivated as a culinary and medicinal plant from India to Indonesia and the Antilles. The hand-sized, fleshy, succulent leaves are very aromatic. They are an important spice in Jamaican cooking, especially for fish. In India this borage is added to beer.

Little attention is paid to wild thyme because it grows by the side of many roads. The taste is very mild and suitable for rustic dishes and herb tea.

The fruity aroma of orange thyme, here in flower. is similar to that of oranges. It is used in sweet dishes and to make tea.

Silver thyme differs from lemon thyme only in color; the taste is exactly the same.

Wild thyme can be used in cooking in the same way as cultivated thyme, but it has a weak flavor.

The spicy aroma of caraway thyme is reminiscent of both caraway and garden thyme. It is a good seasoning for beef.

Green Indian borage leaves have a marked, delicate, and mild thyme flavor that is very pleasant in salads.

This decorative variegated Indian borage has a dryer taste, rather like that of oregano.

When candied, violets and rose petals tranform their perfume into taste. In this way they not only garnish sweet dishes, but also complement the flavor.

○ Kitchen know-how

Cooking with flowers is a refined art form, inspired by the wealth of ideas and creativity of cooks who want to bring a touch of romanticism into the kitchen and on to the plate. Edible flowers can be an optical stimulus for even a simple dish. Many flowers also add a piquant flavor, and some even have healing properties. It is, however, an art form that depends heavily on the time of year. You have to bide your time while the plants grow and develop, until the season to harvest the flowers arrives. Then all you need to do is pick them and use them. For example, the daisies, milfoil, roses, clover, and lavender flowers shown here are all very decorative, and roses, lavender, and violets are also beautifully scented. Woodruff flowers are pretty and smell of vanilla if warmed gently. You should always take care to consume only the flowers of plants that you are absolutely sure are not poisonous.

COOKING WITH FLOWERS

There are very few flowers that are of culinary value because of their taste, such as violets, roses, orange blossom, and nasturtiums. All the other edible flowers are used more for decoration. The purplish-blue flowers of **lavender** (*Lavandula angustifolia*) are picked before they open. The long-stemmed, dark **violet** (*Viola odorata*), and the occasional white or pink flowers are suitable for making tea, vinegar, and as a spice. **Cowslip** (*Caltha palustris*), or marsh marigold, grows in damp meadows, by the edge of streams and in ditches. The creamy-white flower of **black elder** (*Sambucus nigra*) hangs from the branches in umbrella-shaped clusters. Only the petals, preferably the tips, of the daisy-like **chrysanthemum** (*Chrysanthemum coronarium*) flowers are used. Like the leaves, the flowers of the **tangerine marigold** (*Tagetes tenuifolia*) can be used to flavor sweet dishes and fruit drinks. **Dittany-of-Crete** (*Origanum dictamnus*) has delicate pink flowers. **Pansies** (*Viola tricolor*) have yellow, blue, white, and purple flowers with a distinctive marking on a long spur. **Wild roses** (*Rosa dumetorum*) grow to 10 ft high and were previously thought to be a subspecies of the dog rose (*Rosa canina*); they differ from these only in the downy hairs on the leaf stems and the veins on the underside of the leaves. **Sweet orange blossom** (*Citrus sinensis*) is used to make orange blossom water. There are more than 100 varieties and 15,000 cultivated forms of **begonia**. **Beach rocket** (*Cakile maritima*) is also known as European sea mustard. The scarlet-tongued **monarda** (*Monarda didyma*), known also as bee balm and Oswego tea, flowers form heavy heads at the end of the stalks. The **pot marigold** (*Calendula officinalis*) produces brilliantly colored flowers with a crisp texture.

Lavender flowers have a spicy, bitter, aromatic perfume, but this is not as strong as that of the young leaves. They are added to herbes de Provence *for their pretty color.*

Violets *are slightly sharp and a little sweet, but do not have any special taste of their own; they can be candied.*

Marsh marigold *flowers have a spicy aroma. The buds can be used instead of capers.*

Black elder *flower has a spicy sweet scent.*

Chrysanthemums *have a dry, bitter flavor. Flowers that have just come into bloom are less bitter, and can be used as a salad ingredient or as a garnish.*

Tangerine marigold *flowers are spicy and aromatic. Both the flowers and the leaves have a slight citrus aroma..*

The flowers of dittany-of-Crete *clearly taste of marjoram, but with a slightly sweet component.*

The pansy *can be used to flavor vinegar and can also be candied.*

Candied wild roses *can be used as both a flavoring and garnish.*

Sweet orange blossom *has a strong, enticing fragrance, which goes well with sweet and fruit-based dishes.*

Begonias *taste slightly acidic, and can be coated in sugar to make sourballs.*

Beach rocket *has a slightly bitter but spicy taste. The flowers can be used as a salad ingredient.*

Monarda *can be used to make a refreshing lemonade, which is colored pale pink by the flowers.*

Marigold *goes well with dill or chives. The petals were formerly used as a substitute for saffron.*

GROWING CULINARY HERBS YOURSELF

It is easy to grow culinary herbs yourself, and it is well worth doing. If you enjoy cooking, you know that truly fresh herbs impart a unique flavor to foods. Even if you can buy fresh herbs inexpensively, they can never be as fresh as those you pick yourself, and growing your own means you will never be without them when you need them. Cooking and eating are also much more fun when you have grown the herbs yourself. If you do not have a garden, or enough space in it to grow herbs, you can grow them in containers on a patio or balcony, or even in pots on the windowsill. It takes less time, space and effort than you might think to keep yourself supplied with fresh herbs throughout the year.

A FEW BASIC FACTS

There are a few important points you need to observe to keep your herbs happy. In the beginning it is a good idea to plant annual herbs, such as dill, arugula, and basil, between perennials, because it often takes a year for the latter to develop fully. The annuals can easily be grown from seed, along with the biennials parsley and coriander. It is advisable to buy thyme, savory, mint, balm, tarragon, chives, marjoram, and oregano as young plants so you do not have to wait too long to pick your first crop from these perennials. Herbs are useful plants and therefore should be allowed to grow luxuriantly so you can use them again and again. They need a warm, sunny site and good, loose soil with plenty of nutrients. Plants that need a lot of fertilizer are basil, dill, chives, parsley, chervil, and coriander. However, thyme, savory, and mugwort prefer poorer soil. Most other herbs are happy with soil that is somewhere in between. Before planting herbs in the garden, be sure to add some compost or an organo-mineral fertilizer and additional garden lime to the top soil. You can also use garden lime to improve commercial compost for potted plants. Containers, from patio tubs to windowsill pots, should have sufficient openings in the bottom to allow excess water to drain away. In addition to these optimum conditions, you also must have patience, because the plants need time to establish themselves before they are ready to be gathered and used.

OUTDOOR HERBS

All known herbs, including the popular Mediterranean ones, are best cultivated in the garden. However, not all basil is identical, and the same can be said about many herbs: there are different varieties and they each may have a different level of resistance to disease, pests, and weather conditions. You should select the most robust varieties for your garden. So-called wild basil is one such variety, which grows well even in poor

Some gardens that specialize in growing herbs will send out both plants and seeds by mail order. This is a simple and practical way to acquire the plants you want and to find out about new herbs. Many herbs cannot be grown from seeds, or only with difficulty, while rare varieties may not be available locally.

Some herbs, such as mint and tarragon, can be propagated very easily by taking cuttings. Take a couple of strong stalks from a bunch of mint, put them in a glass of water and they will have rooted after 1–2 weeks. Then pot the young plants and gradually introduce them to bright light before putting them in their final location.

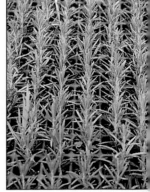

The nursery in a herb center. All annual and many perennial species are propagated from seeds. Some seeds, such as those of basil, must not be covered in soil, or they will not sprout. To prevent the seeds drying out, the boxes can be covered with a fine gravel. They should never be left in direct sunlight: the plants can tolerate strong light only after the seedlings start to turn green. When the first proper leaves start to grow, the plants are separated, so that each plant has a good chance of developing.

Boxes are labeled with an indelible, light-resistant pen. When the plants have been separated, each container is given its own label.

summers. There are also differences in the size of herbs. Plants that are usually quite small, such as thyme, marjoram, and savory, have cultivated varieties that grow taller to make them easier to pick. For your herb garden, you should pick a spot that is quick and easy to get to from the kitchen, even if it is only a tiny area near the patio door! Flowerpots and pottery tubs planted with herbs are particularly decorative and can be positioned in a sheltered spot near the house. In winter they will need additional protection. One reason why monastery gardens in the Middle Ages were surrounded by walls and thick hedges is that herbs, which were grown there extensively, are, more than any other cultivated plants, dependent on protection from wind for growth and quality. The leaves must not be tough if they are to be used raw, and the flavor also develops better in a sheltered site. It is generally thought that the strongest taste develops in a hot summer, in direct sunlight, but this is not always true. Thyme, for example, has a much better flavor in the cooler seasons, and salad burnet develops its nutty cucumber-like taste only after a heavy shower. Both these herbs can be picked throughout the year, as can sage, Welsh onion, savory, mugwort, and wormwood.

HERBS IN THE GREENHOUSE OR CONSERVATORY

In winter a well-lit spot in a greenhouse or conservatory is almost perfect for many herbs, especially if it is not quite as warm as in the rest of the house. Rosemary and lemon verbena, for example, will do well here. Many herbs that do not come from the tropics but still cannot withstand a winter out of doors will easily survive here. The following plants do not like to be kept too warm during the winter: bay, all types of oregano, marjoram, pineapple sage, Greek sage, and myrtle. Otherwise, herbs kept in the conservatory should be treated in the same way as houseplants.

HERBS IN THE HOUSE

There are very few herbs that cannot be grown indoors, at least for a while. Indeed, some of the most popular herbs, such as basil, grow as well indoors as out. Dwarf basil is excellent for this purpose: all you need to do is turn the pot occasionally to ensure all sides of the plant are exposed to natural light. The very attractive red-leafed varieties of basil need even more light than their green-leafed relatives. One big advantage of growing herbs indoors is that they are readily available whatever the weather. The foliage is usually more tender than that of herbs grown outdoors, because of the warmth and lack of wind. However, plants grown in constant warmth grow more quickly, and are often delicate and more prone to disease and pests. If you cannot provide such plants with a cooler location, a small fan may help. A healthy microclimate also requires sufficient humidity, which can easily be achieved by grouping all the pots of herbs together and standing them on a layer of tiny pebbles, capillary matting, or even newspaper that is kept moist. In contrast to the slow-growing, shade-loving tropical plants that are often chosen as houseplants, herbs grow more quickly and therefore need more sun. If the older leaves start to turn yellow, then it is time to add some fertilizer. Problems may arise in winter when the days are shorter and the sunlight is weak. If you still want to have herbs through the winter, you will need to provide additional lighting, in the form of a neon plant light, about 8 in. above the plants. So-called plant lamps that have heating elements are not suitable, because they give off too much heat. Herbs that are used to a cool, brisk climate are not always easy to grow indoors. Savory and thyme, which come from the mountainous, windy areas of southern Europe, can easily fail if they are spoiled by too much warmth. If this happens, tropical and subtropical herbs are a good alternative; for example, Indian borage instead of thyme, or Mexican oregano instead of savory. These herbs contain flavors to which our taste-buds are accustomed, just in a different plant. Most tropical and subtropical varieties can be cultivated indoors in the same conditions required by most other houseplants: a temperature that does not fall below around 60°F, no sudden drafts or changes in temperature, good sunlight, proper watering, and feeding. The kitchen is not always the ideal location for potted herbs, as quick variations in temperature and fumes from cooking can damage the plants.

Short-term storage

If stored in an airtight, plastic container, herbs will keep for a long time in the refrigerator. Even wilted herbs will be dew-fresh again.

If sprayed with water and packed into a tightly closed plastic bag, herbs will keep well stored in the salad crisper in the refrigerator.

The herbs should be loosely layered in the bag and put in the refrigerator with enough space around them so that the tender leaves are not damaged.

PREFERRED LOCATIONS

There are herbs that are suited to the windowsill and those that prefer the outdoors, but some herbs can be grown both indoors and out. It is therefore helpful if you know which plants best suit which location. Here are a few in each category.

Indoor herbs
Bay (*Laurus nobilis*)
Bush basil (*Ocimum basilicum* var. *minimum*)
Indian borage (*Coleus amboinicus*)
Lemon grass (*Cymbopogon citratus*)
Marjoram (*Origanum majorana*)
Mint (*Mentha spicata*)
Myrtle (*Myrtus communis*)
Society garlic (*Tulbaghia violacea*)
Vietnamese coriander (*Polygonum odoratum*)

Outdoor herbs
Chives (*Allium schoenoprasum*)
Flat-leafed parsley (*Petroselium crispum*)
French sorrel (*Rumex scutatus*)
French tarragon (*Artemisia dracunculus* var. *sativa*)
Garden thyme (*Thymus vulgaris*)
Lemon balm (*Melissa officinalis*)
Lovage (*Levisticum officinale*)
Turkish mint (*Mentha spicata* var. *crispa*)
Winter marjoram (*Origanum heracleoticum*)
Winter savory (*Satureja montana*)

GATHERING HERBS

When gathering herbs it is very important that you pick whole sprigs rather than individual leaves. You can also use the flowers. As soon as the dew has evaporated and the flowers open, simply cut off the sprig of herb close to the base. Small flowers, such as lavender blossom, should be picked before they open fully. As a basic principle, the tender leaves and shoots are used in cooking. When picking herbs, whether using scissors, a knife, or your hands, you are also pruning them. You should therefore ensure that you prune the plant evenly. Always grasp the plant carefully so that the delicate leaves are not bruised. If you do not cut too far down, but leave the leaf pair nearest the base, the plant will be able to recover quickly and will grow back bushy. Do not forget to use the tougher leaves, which often have a stronger flavor. Simply cook them with the food and remove them before serving. Herbs that develop tougher leaves are myrtle, savory, bay, thyme, and rosemary. If you dry such tough herbs in a shady place, you can then easily grind them, using a coffee grinder or blender.

Growing and tending fresh herbs provides you with attractive and aromatic plants, which impart a refined and balanced flavor to your food.

The heat of a tiled stove is ideal for drying herbs. The bunches are hung on a pulley positioned at the correct height above the oven.

PRESERVING AND BUYING HERBS

Very few herbs can be bought fresh throughout the year, and not many people who garden for a hobby are lucky enough to be able to pick fresh herbs from their own gardens through the winter. If you do not want to go without your favorite herbs at any time of year, and do not want to rely on the small containers of dried herbs in the store, then you can lay in your own supply of herbs.

Freezing herbs

Fresh herbs can be frozen, individually or in mixes, in plastic boxes or bags. The finely chopped herbs can then be removed a spoonful at a time.

Herb ice cubes are a practical way of dividing herbs into portions. Put the prepared herbs, individual or mixed, into an ice-cube tray and cover with water or stock.

When packed separately and labeled, the frozen ice cubes can easily be stored in the freezer. They are ideal for adding directly to sauces and soups.

OIL, VINEGAR AND SALT

The oldest method of preserving herbs is to cover them in oil, vinegar, or salt. The fresh herbs are finely chopped or puréed, packed into wide-necked bottles or screw-top jars and covered with white vinegar or good quality oil, until the liquid covers the herbs to a finger's width. It is important to use a good oil that will not become rancid quickly — good quality olive oil always

It is easy to preserve herbs in oil and in vinegar. If possible, use opaque containers rather than clear glass.

Think very carefully before preserving herbs in salt: this method should be used only for herbs to be added to dishes that require a correspondingly salty note.

running water and then drain or shake them to get rid of the excess water, and spread them out on paper towels to dry completely. Depending on their intended use, the herbs can be prepared in a number of ways: separated into individual leaves, chopped, or even puréed in a mixer. They can be packed in foil, freezer bags or boxes, even in small, used yogurt containers. One practical method is to freeze them in ice-cube trays, so that you have small quantities available. If it is too time-consuming for you to chop them, you can freeze the herbs on a tray for about three hours, then crumble them, put them in containers, and return them to the freezer. Herbs can be frozen individually or in mixes. Frozen herbs are simple to use. They do not have to be defrosted and, using a sharp knife, you can scrape them off a solid block straight into the cooking food. Preserve herbs according to the season, and label with the date of freezing as well as the name of the herb.

DRYING

The most common method of preserving herbs is still drying. Drying means removing the water content, thus putting a stop to the bacteria that cause rot and mold. At the same time the dried herbs shrink and, when appropriately packed, take up little space. However, some herbs are not suited to this method, losing almost all their flavor. Basil, mugwort, savory,

works well. Herbs are preserved in salt in layers: one part salt to four parts coarsely chopped herbs. The containers should be airtight and stored in a cool, dark place (not the refrigerator). Of these three processes, herbs preserved in oil have the most neutral taste for later use. The leftover oil can also be used as a seasoning. The vinegar is best used in salads. This way of preserving herbs should not be confused with making flavored oil and vinegar as shown on page 135. When preserved in salt, herbs lose some of their flavor, and can be used only sparingly because of the high salt content.

FREEZING

Freezing is a popular method of preserving herbs.. When frozen, herbs, like other foods, retain their flavor, vitamins and color exceptionally well. It is essential that herbs to be frozen are absolutely fresh. If possible, pick herbs in the morning and freeze them immediately. If necessary, wash them briefly under

Herb ice cubes should added to hot liquid without being defrosted.

Drying herbs

Large quantities of herbs or flowers can be dried on a wooden trellis, in warm, dry air, but not in direct sunlight.

Drying herbs in the microwave is quick and easy. Cover a dish with paper towels, scatter a few herbs on top, and cover lightly with more paper towels.

The paper absorbs the moisture. The drying time depends on the strength of the herbs and the amount of water they contain. It usually takes between 1 and 4 minutes.

Small dried leaves can easily be stripped from the stems. Larger leaves can also be crumbled.

Peppermint develops a sharper taste when dried, because of its high menthol content, and must be used with care.

Mint is an ideal culinary herb for drying. Only the leaves are used.

Mugwort retains its flavor when dried. Although the leaves are very aromatic, it is mostly the flowers that are used.

Basil loses its flavor when dried. The best preservation method is freezing.

Sage should be picked and dried when the flowers open. Only the leaves are used as a seasoning.

dill, lavender, lovage, marjoram, varieties of mint, oregano, wild thyme, rosemary, sage, garden thyme, and hyssop are suitable for home drying. The easiest way to dry herbs is to use the natural warmth of the sun, but not direct sunlight, because strong light evaporates the essential oils and fades the leaves. Drying is best done in the shade of a covered terrace or balcony, in a dry, well-ventilated cupboard, or in the warmth of the oven, but not in a garage contaminated with exhaust fumes. If possible, avoid washing the freshly picked herbs. Tie them together in little bunches by the stems, then hang them up in a well-aired place, not too close together. For blossoming herbs, such as lavender, it is a good idea to spread paper under the bunch to collect the dried flowers when they fall. Do not cover them with a paper bag, as is sometimes recommended, as this slows down the drying process, which also means the herbs will become more discolored. Instead of tying them up in bunches, you can spread the herbs loosely on a sheet of paper, a wooden trellis, or a frame covered with a porous fabric, such as muslin or nylon net; never try to dry herbs on a wire mesh, as metal is damaging to them. Good ventilation is essential for drying herbs by either method. In wet or cool summers it is possible to dry the herbs in a cooling oven. The temperature should not exceed 95°F and the oven door should be left slightly ajar to let the moisture escape. You can also dry herbs in the microwave. Wash them, divide them into small sprigs, and place them loosely between two paper towels. Dry them in small quantities with the turntable in the highest position, checking the setting each time. The herbs are dry when the leaves crumble between your fingers. You can then strip off the leaves and, depending on the variety, rub them between your hands or crush them with a rolling pin to give a coarse or fine consistency. Pack the dried herbs into clean, dry jars — opaque if possible — and close tightly. Plastic containers are not suitable because of the condensation that forms. You now have a year's supply of herbs. It is very easy to revive the flavor of dried herbs. Depending on the recipe, leave the herbs to soak in stock, wine, or water, or spray lightly with water and heat briefly (5 seconds) in the microwave. When using dried herbs, remember that 1 teaspoon of dried herbs is equal to roughly 3 teaspoons of fresh herbs.

KEEPING HERBS FRESH

Freshly picked or bought herbs are not always used immediately. To keep them fresh during warm weather or for a few days before you use them, put the washed, drained herbs loosely in a plastic food bag and keep it in the salad compartment in the refrigerator. Herbs with long, firm stalks can be washed, shaken dry, and put in a glass filled with water, then wrapped loosely in plastic wrap and put in the refrigerator.

Dill loses only a little of its flavor when dried. However, freezing is still the best method of preserving dill.

Marjoram increases in flavor when dried, becoming more powerful and sharper.

Winter savory should always be picked and dried before it begins to flower.

Lavender flowers retain their attractive color when dried. For this reason they are included in herb mixes, although they add very little in the way of flavor.

Oregano should be picked and dried just before flowering. It does not lose its flavor.

Lemon balm should be dried in a dark place if you want it to retain some color. It loses hardly any flavor.

Lovage should be used as sparingly dried as fresh.

Hyssop should be used only in small quantities even when dried, because of its strong taste.

Lemon thyme smells strongly of lemon even when dried. It should be picked as soon as the flowers open.

Thyme, when dried, becomes a slightly more powerful seasoning than the fresh herb.

Savory retains its peppery flavor well when dried.

Dried rosemary can be used in the same way as the fresh herb.

BUYING HERBS

Vegetable markets, greengrocers, fancy food stores, and even supermarkets offer a steadily increasing choice of fresh herbs. Whether grown outdoors or in greenhouses, locally or imported, the most common types are available throughout the year. They should be bought in the morning to ensure that they are as fresh as possible. The stalks should be firm and the leaves should be neither wilted nor bruised. Mail-order catalogs from growers may offer a good opportunity to familiarize yourself with new herbs; their addresses can be found in gardening and cooking magazines. Industry offers a range of herbs to meet the requirements of any consumer. Frozen herbs and mixtures of herbs are the best alternative to the fresh product. They are considered to be the best quality preserved, and retain their color and flavor, as well as the vitamins and minerals. However, they are relatively expensive and the range is fairly small. On the other hand, the range of dried herbs is incredibly wide. Even commercially dried herbs should be kept for only a year, so look out for the packaging date or "best by" date. When buying dried herbs, choose whole leaves in preference to rubbed or chopped herbs, as the former do not lose their flavor as quickly as the latter. Dried herbs should be strongly colored and should be stored in a dark, dry place that is as cool as possible. They should be crushed or ground in a mortar only just before use. The flavor can be revived if they are left to soak in a little stock, wine, or water.

Fines herbes, a classic of French cooking, must include parsley, chives, chervil, and tarragon.

As with any fresh produce, it is important to choose the best quality of herbs when buying them. Look for strong color and healthy leaves, and check that they smell and taste as they should.

HERB MIXES

There is a culinary tradition of combining specific herbs to create a very special flavor, as is the case with *fines herbes* and *herbes de Provence*, for example. Ideally, fresh herbs should be used. They are added in a bunch to the dish and removed before serving. The range of commercial dried mixtures exceeds the wildest dreams, but the basic principle that one typical, dominant flavor should not be buried under too many different seasonings is increasingly forgotten in the rush to produce ever more exotic combinations. If you know your individual herbs and their uses, it is easy to say no to dried mixtures that are difficult to define. The following standard mixtures should have a place in every kitchen.

Bouquet garni This selection of herbs originated in France and is used in salads, soups, sauces, stocks, and consommés. It includes parsley, celery leaf, onion, and thyme, to which savory, basil, tarragon, chervil, dill, salad burnet, rosemary, garlic, and bay can be added.

Fines herbes Another French mixture, *fines herbes* is a combination of equal quantities of parsley, tarragon, chervil, and chives. However, it is not unusual for other herbs, such as sage, basil, savory, thyme, oregano, rosemary, marjoram, lavender, and hyssop to be included. Both fresh and dried mixtures are suitable for seasoning meat, game, and poultry dishes, soups and

There are dried herb mixtures to suit every taste, and they come in every size, from little jars for household use to large quantities for catering and the food industry. The consumer is spoiled for choice, from *herbes de Provence* to *herbs for pizza* to special combinations for meats, seafood, and salads.

sauces, as well as any dish to which herbs are frequently added, for example egg dishes, cream cheese, cheese, and butter.

Herbes de Provence This famous mixture from the south of France is made up of a similar combination to that used in *fines herbes*, but aniseed and lavender are included instead of sage and parsley. Oregano, hyssop, basil, savory, and thyme can also be present. The mixture is suitable for meat and barbecued dishes, sauces, vegetable soups, game, and poultry.

Frankfurt green sauce herbs Dominated by parsley, chives, borage, cress, salad burnet, dill, and sorrel, this sauce is used primarily for egg, fish, and meat dishes.

Salad dressing herbs The individual flavor of the salad should not be overpowered or changed by the herb mixture, but should be emphasized by it. There are numerous mixtures on the market that are similar to *fines herbes* or *herbes de Provence*, but also include seasonings such as pepper, capers, lemon zest, caraway, and mustard seed.

Herb vinegars The most important components in the mixtures are basil, savory, dill, tarragon, parsley, peppercorns, thyme, garlic, and horseradish. The quantity of herb to be used varies between $1/3$ and $3^1/2$ oz per quart of vinegar, depending on the strength of flavor required.

There is no need to buy dried herbes de Provence or other mixtures when you can easily make them yourself from fresh herbs. Since there is no single recipe for these classic mixtures you can vary the basic ingredients and their proportions to suit yourself. Whether you dry, freeze or preserve them in oil, you will have a supply of your preferred mixture ready at your fingertips.

COOKING WITH HERBS

Good cooks treat the foods with which they work with the greatest care and respect. Everything has its limitations, but also its hidden secrets, and a good cook has to know both. The difference between everyday cooking and a culinary masterpiece is not necessarily a result of different main ingredients. The reason that the meals of both the Chinese emperor a thousand years BC and the French Sun King, more than 2,600 years later, were considered gastronomic wonders had nothing to do with the basic ingredients — fruits and vegetables of the field and garden, and seafood and meat — but the way in which these simple items were seasoned with whatever could be used to enhance the flavor — the leaves, flowers and roots of herbs. If you are lucky, you can quickly run out into the garden and pick herbs straight from the ground, or from containers on the patio or pots on the windowsill. If you have protected your herbs from insects and pests, you will be picking a mass of flavor. There are many ways, both time-honored and brand new, of preserving these flavors. Many of them are so closely linked with specific recipes that they can neither be criticized nor brought up to date. In the final analysis the same applies to herbs as to wine: we all have to discover for ourselves what we like best. Everyone should work with herbs, to discover their splendid aromas and the wonderful flavors they can impart to even the most simple foods.

If you are a newcomer to herbs or want to expand the range you use, it is a good idea to stick to a few tried and tested varieties, and then gradually try a few more unusual ones, rather than buying modern herb mixtures in fantastic packaging, which quickly lose their essential oils. If you are using dried herbs, buy small amounts of single herbs, perhaps trying different ones on several occasions. If you are buying fresh herbs and do not use them immediately, keep them as fresh as possible. If you stick parsley in a glass of water like a bunch of flowers and forget about it, you turn it into just another green plant. If you chop your parsley in the morning, but do not sprinkle it on your salad until the evening, then you deserve what you get, and finally, if you think parsley is the be all and end all of herbs, you are about to discover a wider world of flavors and aromas.

In the following chapters we have brought together the culinary knowledge of the old and new worlds as it has been combined and expanded in the course of history, in the aftermath of conquests and along caravan routes, by sailing ships and the wedding gifts of noble ladies, and by every curious traveler. If you want to learn how the spices of the Far East can transform the simple carrot into a genuine delicacy; if you would like to know how to create a new taste sensation every day by adding aromatic herbs to oil or butter to enhance a salad or a dish of pasta, then you will surely study this section with enthusiasm and passion.

CREATIVE WAYS WITH HERBS AND GARLIC

Have the courage to experiment and think about how you use herbs. Just as with everything else, there is a right way and a wrong way to treat herbs. First, wash herbs thoroughly under lukewarm, not hot or cold, running water, because you cannot assume that they have been grown in absolutely clean air. Next, either leave them to dry in layers on paper towels or use paper towels to pat them dry. Then chop them as required. With the exception of savory, thyme, and rosemary, whole sprigs of fresh herbs are rarely cooked with food. Usually the leaves or flowers are stripped from the stalks and reduced in size in some way. In addition to traditional chopping techniques using knife, chopper or scissors (see illustrations below), there are also machines to do the job, sometimes hand-operated (herb mill), sometimes electric (food processor). Machines produce results quickly, but sometimes the herbs are thoroughly mashed by the fast action. This may be all right when the herbs are to be used in sauces or fillings, but not when they are meant to be easy to taste and see, which is usually the case. A pestle and mortar are indispensable when herbs have to be mixed with other seasonings or ingredients. Pesto (see pages 76–7) is a good example of this, and also a perfect example of how an individual herb, in this case basil, can dominate in flavor. There are other herbs that have the same effect, such as savory, rosemary, or tarragon, for which reason they appear in mixtures of fresh herbs only occasionally.

You have to learn the proper way to work with herbs. Italian cuisine has always been a superb example of this, and students at the Instituto Professionale di Stato per i Servizi Alberghieri e della Ristorazione in Finale Ligure, under the leadership of chef Signore Giovanni Pizzocri, go about it with enthusiasm and are proof that cooking in Italy still begins with herbs. The bigger the knife, the better, as the students practice chopping herbs evenly and finely.

Chopping herbs

With a knife, it is easy to select the size of cut required. A knife is best for use with large-leafed herbs, which can be held together easily.

A chopper is an easy way to finely chop small-leafed herbs quickly and easily. It is the best tool to use for curly parsley.

Using scissors is an easy way to chop small quantities directly into the bowl or pan. It is important to dry the herbs thoroughly after washing them.

A BUNDLE OF TASTE

Sprigs of very fresh herbs are used, tied up in bunches, in stock, consommés, sauces and wherever a lot of cooking liquid is used. In this way they are able to release their full flavor, and later can easily be removed. The classic bouquet garni for fine sauces, stocks, and gravy consists of one sprig of thyme, a bay leaf, and three stalks of parsley. Of course, this combination is not always suitable. The bunches of herbs shown on the right (with vegetables) are specially tailored to specific stocks and gravies.

Bouquet garni for poultry is based on parsley, tarragon, and scallion, with a carrot and piece of fennel.

Bouquet garni for fish stock is made of tarragon and thyme in roughly equal proportions, lots of parsley, celeriac, and a few celery leaves. To this is added the thinly peeled rind of half a lemon and, for a hot flavor, half a chili pepper, deseeded.

A universal bouquet garni for meat is composed of turnip-rooted, or Hamburg, parsley , a clove of garlic, a carrot, lots of parsley, lovage, lemon thyme, oregano, and just one sprig of savory (more would add too much acidity).

If you want beef or game to be heavily flavored combine a scallion, turnip-rooted, or Hamburg, parsley, celery leaves, parsley, a small sprig of rosemary, thyme, sage leaves, two bay leaves, and the thinly peeled rind of half an orange in a spicy bouquet.

SAUCES AND BUTTERS

"If you can make a good sauce, then you're a good cook" so the saying goes, for in this way you can turn a simple accompaniment or a modest main dish into an epicure's delight.

Many of the classic sauces we use today are traditional recipes, such as pesto from Italy, aïoli from France, green sauce from Germany, and mint sauce from England, which are associated with their country of origin rather than an individual chef. We have already noted that herbs were first widely cultivated by monks, who used them for both medicinal and culinary purposes. At first herbs intended to infuse a dish were ground with the meat in a pestal and mortar, the food processor of the day. Soon the monks learned to make green sauces from freshly picked culinary herbs to accompany the fish and egg dishes served on their many meatless days. These sauces had to be used immediately, unless the green paste was mixed with salt or oil. This was the forerunner of pesto. Later, the introduction of sieve and scales changed the method of processing these short-lived ingredients, and sauces based on different herbs to accompany specific types of food were gradually incorporated into domestic cooking. One green sauce, from Frankfurt, has become famous throughout the world. In what is believed to be the original recipe, found in the handwritten recipe book of a wealthy merchant's wife, herbs were carefully weighed, passed through a sieve with a mixture of crushed, hard-cooked egg yolks, vinegar, mustard and oil, pepper and salt, and then mixed with sour cream. When the recipe appeared in published cookbooks for the first time, probably in the mid-nineteenth century, an abbreviated form was suggested in which the herbs were simply mixed with mayonnaise, but the original recipe is the one that was favored and has endured. Perhaps similar stories could also be told about the other famous herb sauces presented here.

SALSA VERDE

As is often the case with classic dishes, there is a basic recipe for what is one of the most well-known Italian herb sauces, and then there are many variations, often to the detriment of the original. The main ingredient in every case is fresh parsley, with garlic, capers, extra virgin olive oil, and some fresh white breadcrumbs softened in a little stock. With the exception of salt and pepper, any other ingredients are variations. Cooks in northern Italy have a flexible attitude towards salsa verde. It does not matter to them whether spices, gherkins, and peppers are added, as in Piedmont, or sieved egg yolk and finely chopped egg white are folded in right at the end, as in the Veneto; this sauce may always taste diffrent, but it always tastes good. The true flavor develops especially well in combination with hot meats, and is also excellent with poached fish and boiled vegetables.

4 cups fresh parsley
1 clove garlic
$4^{1}/_{2}$ tsp salted capers
$^{1}/_{2}$ cup shallots
$^{1}/_{2}$ cup chopped pickled gherkins
2 tbsp fresh white breadcrumbs
$^{1}/_{2}$ tsp salt
freshly ground white pepper
2 tbsp balsamic vinegar
1 cup olive oil

Wash the parsley, drain well, and pat with paper towels so that it is as dry as possible. Remove the large stems and finely chop the leaves with a knife. Chop the clove of garlic very finely. Chop capers and shallots a little more roughly. Mix everything together in a bowl with the pickled gherkins and breadcrumbs, and season to taste with salt and pepper. Stir in the vinegar. Pour in the olive oil in a thin stream, as you would if making mayonnaise, and stir. The quantity will depend on the preferred consistency of the sauce. For a lighter variation, add $^{1}/_{2}$–$^{2}/_{3}$ cup yogurt before adding the oil.

Pesto and Pistou

A taste combination dominated by garlic and basil, these two variations on a theme cannot be beaten for popularity, not just in their Ligurian and Provençal homes, but throughout the world.

Although the Genoese basil sauce pesto is known chiefly as a sauce for pasta, it is also eaten with boiled vegetables and with lamb. The main ingredients, in addition to basil, are garlic, pine nuts, olive oil, and, of course, cheese, which determines how strong the sauce tastes. If mature pecorino cheese is used, the flavor is strong; if Parmesan is used, the flavor is milder. The following recipe, which uses both cheeses, achieves a delicate balance. Pine nuts are omitted from Provençal pistou. Instead, tomato is sometimes added, which gives the sauce a pleasant, fresh taste. Both sauces should be used as fresh as possible to make the most of the basil flavor (the *fino verde* type is best; see page 41). If you want to enjoy pesto outside the season for fresh basil, keep a supply in the freezer. In making pesto for freezing it is important to use only a little olive oil and to omit the cheese. The remaining oil and cheese can be added when the pesto is defrosted. It will then taste like freshly made sauce.

PESTO ALLA GENOVESE

Whether or not the Genoans really did create this basil sauce has little bearing on international menus. What matters is that this sauce exists. Its adaptability is demonstrated throughout the Riviera, where it is served with an enormous range of dishes.

4 cups fresh basil
4 cloves garlic
$1/2$ cup pine nuts, $1/2$ tsp salt
$1/2$ cup each freshly grated pecorino and Parmesan cheeses
up to $5/8$ cup extra virgin olive oil

Wash the basil, dry thoroughly and chop coarsely. Peel the garlic cloves and chop coarsely. If liked, toast the pine nuts in the oven to increase the flavor. Prepare the pesto as shown in the illustrations. The consistency of the finished sauce should be similar to that of mayonnaise. If the pesto is to be used with pasta, add 3 tablespoons of boiling, salted water from the pasta to it. **Trenette col pesto alla genovese.** Pesto first became famous in combination with these narrow ribbons of pasta, which are served *al dente*. To make this classic dish, peel 6 oz potatoes and cut into small dice. Clean 1/3 cup green beans. Cook both in boiling salted water until they are just done and retain some bite. Remove from the cooking liquid and keep warm. Now cook 9 oz trenette in the same liquid until *al dente*, then drain. Mix the potatoes, green beans, and trenette with 1 recipe of pesto and 2 tablespoons grated pecorino cheese. Garnish with basil and serve immediately.

PISTOU

The Provençal basil sauce is the classic accompaniment to the famous vegetable soup from this region. In Haute Provence pistou is prepared with tomatoes instead of pine nuts, which makes the sauce pleasantly acidic and gives the soup a fresher taste.

3 cloves garlic
1¹/₂ cups fresh basil
2 tomatoes
¹/₂ tsp salt
1 cup freshly grated Parmesan cheese
4–5 tbsp good quality olive oil

Coarsely chop the garlic. Wash and dry the basil, and remove stems. Using a knife or kitchen scissors, cut the leaves into strips. Place the tomatoes under a hot broiler, remove the skins and seeds, and chop the flesh into large dice. Finely crush the garlic using a pestle and mortar, then add the basil and salt, and crush to form a paste. Add the cheese and diced tomato a bit at a time and work into the mixture thoroughly. Gradually add the olive oil and continue stirring until the sauce is the consistency of smooth, thick cream. Serve straight from the mortar to accompany *soupe au pistou*.

To make the *soupe au pistou*, add 2 diced potatoes, 2 firm tomatoes, skinned and deseeded, 2 chopped leeks and a few chopped celery leaves to 9 cups boiling, salted water. Add freshly ground pepper, cover the pot, and simmer gently for about 2 hours. Then add 3 cups each canned or cooked kidney and small white beans, 1 lb green beans, cut into short sticks, 1 lb sliced zucchini and 1 cup rigatoni pasta and cook for 15 minutes or until done. Mix a few spoonfuls of the soup stock with the pistou. The sauce should never be cooked, so add it to the soup after serving.

Preparing pesto

Pound the peeled garlic, pine nuts, and salt in the mortar.

Add the coarsely chopped basil to the garlic mixture and crush to a fine paste.

Gradually add the finely grated cheeses and stir in carefully.

Add the olive oil in a trickle, as if making mayonnaise, and stir in well.

To preserve pesto pour it into a glass jar and top with a thin layer of olive oil. When tightly closed, the pesto will keep for over 1 week in the refrigerator.

PARSLEY PURÉE

Simple but stylish, this fresh sauce goes well with any dish that has an affinity for parsley, especially meat and pasta.

2¹/₂ cups curly parsley, 2¹/₂ cups flat-leaf parsley
¹/₄ cup chopped shallots
1¹/₂ tbsp butter, 1¹/₄ cups light cream
¹/₂ tsp salt, freshly ground white pepper
3 tbsp whipped cream

Wash the parsley, strip the leaves from the stems, blanch quickly, and refresh immediately in ice-cold water. Drain well, pat dry with paper towels and chop finely. Gently fry the chopped shallots in the butter until soft and transparent. Add the parsley and cream, and bring to the boil. Boil until reduced to half the quantity, then purée in a blender or food processor. Season to taste with salt and pepper. Finally, fold the whipped cream into the purée.

Only aromatic French tarragon is suitable for Salsa al Dragoncello; Russian tarragon would be too bitter.

Purées and sauces

Based on just one herb, these special seasonings have a purity of flavor.

SALSA AL DRAGONCELLO

This tarragon sauce from Italy is usually served with stewed beef. It can also be served with *bollito misto* or baked fish.

2 slices white bread
$^1\!/_2$ cup good quality olive oil
3 cloves garlic
2 tbsp chopped French tarragon
2 tbsp red wine vinegar, 1 tsp balsamic vinegar
salt, freshly ground white pepper

Slice the bread thinly, put into a large dish and pour the oil over it. Finely chop the garlic and sprinkle over the bread with the tarragon. Cover the dish with plastic wrap and leave to marinate for 1–2 hours. Add the two vinegars, salt, and pepper, and purée in a food processor or using a fine meshed sieve. If necessary, the sauce can be thinned down with meat or fish stock.

SPICY CELERY SAUCE

The spicy flavor in this herb sauce comes from freshly ground pepper, which should be added to taste. The sauce goes particularly well with stewed meat.

2 tbsp beef marrow
5 tbsp white breadcrumbs, without crusts
1 cup veal stock
3 tbsp chopped celery
freshly ground white pepper
$^1\!/_2$ tsp salt

Chop the marrow into small dice and heat in a large frying pan. Add the breadcrumbs and fry until brown, stirring constantly. Add the veal stock and bring to the boil several times. Then stir in the celery, add pepper until preferred spiciness is achieved, and season to taste with salt.

WATERCRESS SAUCE

This refreshing, sharp sauce goes well with roast pork.

4 tbsp finely chopped watercress (leaves only, no stems)
1 tbsp white breadcrumbs, without crusts
$^1\!/_2$ cup plain yogurt
1 tsp hot mustard
1 tsp chopped, salted capers
1 chili pepper, deseeded and very finely chopped
$^1\!/_2$ tsp salt
2–3 tbsp whipped cream (optional)

Mix the chopped cress with the breadcrumbs. Stir in the other ingredients, except the whipped cream, to form a paste. Finally stir in the whipped cream and serve chilled.

BASIL PURÉE

In the south of France *purée de basilic* (in the mortar, left) is part of everyday cuisine. Prepared when fresh basil is available, the purée provides a refined seasoning at all times of the year. There is no need for a formal recipe, because the purée is extremely simple to prepare. Wash, dry carefully, chop coarsely, and then pound fresh basil leaves to a fine pulp in a mortar. Add best-quality olive oil in a thin stream and stir until the mixture has the consistency of a thick sauce. Season lightly with salt, if wished, and pour into small glass preserving jars. Pour a thin layer of oil on top and close tightly. The purée is also good used fresh, although you need to use less of it than fresh basil leaves, and it will keep for months.

Guaranteed garlic-free

Not many herb sauces are made without garlic, simply because it combines so well with herbs, but here are some excellent ones.

VIENNESE CHIVE SAUCE

This classic sauce for stewed beef is also served with other dishes; it goes especially well with *fondue bourguignon*. The chives should be as fresh as possible, because although this sauce appears to keep well in the refrigerator, the flavor dissipates very quickly, and when this happens it just tastes sharp.

3 slices white bread, crusts removed,
about 1 cup milk
yolks of 2 hard-cooked eggs, 2 raw egg yolks
$1/2$ tsp salt, freshly ground white pepper
dash of vinegar, $1/4$ tsp tarragon mustard
pinch of sugar, $1 1/4$ cups sunflower oil
3 tbsp finely snipped chives

Soften the bread in the milk, drain well, and pass through a sieve with the hard-cooked egg yolks. Add the raw egg yolks and seasonings, and mix in a food processor. Add the oil a few drops at a time at first, as for mayonnaise, then increase the flow to a thin stream and blend the mixture to a thick, creamy sauce. Stir in the chives just before serving.

FRANKFURT GREEN SAUCE

This herb sauce is like many famous dishes: every cook has his or her "original" recipe for it. No matter how the recipes may differ, however, the basic ingredients are always the same, and the combination of at least eight different herbs reflects either the creativity of the cook or what the stores have to offer. You cannot go wrong with this recipe as long as you use equal quantities of parsley and chives, and smaller amounts of the strongly flavored herbs, such as tarragon and lovage. In this version of the recipe cream and yogurt are used in equal proportions to give the sauce a light, fresh taste.

a good handful of herbs (parsley, chives, dill, chervil, sorrel,
salad burnet, borage, tarragon, lovage)
2 tbsp very finely chopped onion
4 tbsp mild wine vinegar, 4 hard-cooked eggs
$1/2$ cup light cream, $1/2$ cup yogurt
$1/2$ tsp salt, freshly ground white pepper
1 tsp hot mustard, 4 tbsp sunflower oil

Wash and dry the herbs, and chop them very finely. Put them in a bowl with the onions and pour the vinegar over them. Cover and leave to stand for 30 minutes. Shell the eggs and chop finely. Mix the cream and yogurt with the eggs, salt, pepper, and mustard, and gradually add the oil, stirring all the time. Finally, thoroughly mix the cream sauce with the herbs and vinegar, cover and leave in the refrigerator for 30 minutes. Mix the sauce well before serving.

KING EDWARD'S SAUCE

This is a very savory English version of Frankfurt green sauce.

1 cup herbs (equal quantities of tarragon, chervil, salad
burnet and chives)
4 salted whole anchovies, 4 hard-cooked eggs
1 tbsp capers, 1 tbsp Dijon mustard
$1 3/4$ cups olive oil, 5 tbsp tarragon vinegar

Blanch the herbs and pat dry thoroughly with paper towels. Wash, bone, rinse, and dry the anchovies thoroughly. Blend the herbs, anchovies, eggs, capers, and mustard to a paste in a mortar. Gradually add the oil, then the vinegar, stirring all the time. Pass the sauce through a fine sieve.

Mint sauce can lend a fresh flavor to salads where a sweet note is required. Simply substitute mint sauce for some of the vinegar in the salad dressing.

MINT SAUCE

Almost everyone enjoys mint sauce with roast or broiled lamb. If you prefer the sauce sweeter, add half the vinegar to start with, then gradually add more to taste.

$3^1/_2$ cups freshly picked mint
$^3/_8$ cup brown sugar
$^1/_2$ cup good quality wine vinegar
6 tbsp water
2 tsp lemon juice
$^1/_4$ tsp salt

Wash the mint leaves, pat dry with paper towels, chop coarsely, and crush to a fine paste in a mortar with half the sugar. Boil the remaining sugar with the vinegar, water, and lemon juice until the liquid turns clear. Add the crushed mint, season with salt, and leave to cool. The sauce can be passed through a sieve or served with the leaves, as preferred.

Frankfurt green sauce, above, and King Edward's sauce, left, are both ideal with stewed meat dishes, as well as with vegetables and hard-cooked eggs.

Garlic sauces

Of the many garlic sauces, aïoli and rouille, from Provence, are probably the most well known, and perhaps the best. In any case, you simply cannot have bouillabaisse without one of them. They also go well with lamb and with baked potatoes. The milder aïoli takes its flavor mainly from the garlic and salt, while rouille gets its heat and characteristic taste from red chilies and saffron.

AÏOLI

Garlic-lovers simply cannot resist mildly spicy aïoli!

(for 6–8 portions)
6–8 garlic cloves
$\frac{1}{2}$ tsp coarse sea salt
2 slices white bread, crusts removed
$\frac{1}{2}$ cup milk
1 egg yolk
1 cup good quality olive oil
lemon juice

Peel and halve the garlic. Put in a mortar with the sea salt and grind finely. Soften the bread in the milk, squeeze out thoroughly and add to the mortar with the egg yolk. Stir into the garlic and salt mixture until a smooth paste forms. If the paste is too thick, add warm water and stir to a smooth, creamy consistency. Leave the mixture to rest a while. Stir thoroughly again and transfer to a bowl. Stirring constantly, add the olive oil drop by drop, gradually increasing the flow to a thin stream. Season to taste with lemon juice

Variation To transform this classic aïoli into a savory herb sauce with a strong garlic flavor, add 2 tablespoons chopped, fresh, strong-flavored herbs, such as basil, nasturtium, thyme, rosemary, savory, or lovage.

ROUILLE

This piquant and aromatic paste is a special seasoning for fish soups.

1 red pepper
2 hot red chilies
5–6 garlic cloves
1 medium-sized floury potato
$\frac{1}{2}$ tsp coarse sea salt
5–6 threads saffron
1 egg yolk
$\frac{5}{8}$ cup best quality olive oil

Cut the pepper into quarters and remove seeds and core. Cut the chilies in half and carefully remove seeds and core. (Be careful not to get the juice from the chili on your skin or in your eyes.) Peel the garlic and cut each clove in half. Boil the potato in its skin. Prepare the rouille according to the method illustrated.

How to prepare rouille
Blanch the pepper, remove the skin, and cut into small pieces. Grind in a mortar with the prepared chilies, garlic, salt, and saffron. Peel the boiled potato, add to the mortar and work in carefully using the pestle.

Add the egg yolk and stir in. Transfer the paste to a bigger mixing bowl.

How to prepare aïoli

Pound the softened bread and the egg yolk into the garlic and salt mixture. Leave the paste to rest so that the salt has time to dissolve.

Add the oil a few drops at a time, gradually increasing to a thin stream, stirring thoroughly all the time.

Put the mixture into a bowl and add the oil, stirring all the time, until a thick sauce forms. Season to taste with lemon juice.

Continue stirring until the sauce has the consistency of mayonnaise. If you use the finest quality olive oil, success will be guaranteed.

How to prepare herb butter
Rinse the herbs in cold water and shake thoroughly to drain off excess water. Lay them on a dish towel and pat dry completely. Chop finely with a chopper or very sharp knife.

Classic herb butter mixtures
(from left to right): Maître d'hotel, chive butter in a roll, and Montpellier butter. If the butters have been prepared in advance and stored in the refrigerator, bring them up to room temperature before serving. Only then can the delicate flavor of the herbs develop fully.

Classic herb butters

Mixed with butter, herbs are very popular as a finishing touch to soups and sauces, and as a flavorful addition to all grilled and broiled foods, and on freshly toasted or baked bread. The composition and taste is determined by the appropriate ingredients. Use a serrated knife to slice rolls of herb butter into attractive little portions for garnishes. Various types of herb butter can be stored side by side in ice-cubes trays. Prepared butter can be kept in the refrigerator for a maximum of 1 week.

Beat the softened butter until smooth, but not fluffy. Mix in the shallots, garlic, lime juice and seasoning.

Add the herbs and stir in, but not for too long, or the herb juices will discolor the butter.

Allow the herb butter to set a little, put on to waxed paper and carefully shape into a roll. Refrigerate.

MAÎTRE D'HÔTEL BUTTER

6 tbsp parsley, 11 tbsp butter, softened
2 garlic cloves, crushed
2 tbsp lemon juice
salt, freshly ground white pepper

Prepare as described on the left. Serve slices of this butter with broiled or grilled steaks, sole, and any white fish. As variations, dill can be added instead of parsley for pan-fried fish, mint for lamb and rabbit, and sage for liver.

CHIVE BUTTER

4 tbsp chives, 11 tbsp butter, softened
1 tsp lemon juice
1 tsp grated lemon zest
salt, freshly ground white pepper
4 tbsp finely snipped chives for rolling

Prepare the butter as described on the left, then roll in chives so that it is completely covered. This butter is an excellent garnish for any food that goes well with chives — meat, fish, vegetables, and bread.

MONTPELLIER BUTTER

$^3/_4$ cup each watercress and leaf spinach, $^1/_2$ cup each parsley and chervil
3 anchovy fillets, soaked in water or milk
$^1/_4$ cup pickled gherkins, $4^1/_2$ tsp capers
1 clove garlic, 11 tbsp butter, softened
$1^1/_2$ tsp Dijon mustard, 4 tbsp olive oil
1 tsp lemon juice
salt, freshly ground white pepper

Prepare the herbs as described on the left. Finely chop the other ingredients and stir into the butter with the herbs and mustard. Gradually stir in the oil. Season to taste. This mixture is a classic for broiled or grilled fish.

The careful chef *demands the finest quality herbs.*

CÔTE D'AZUR BUTTER

For this attractive, colorful butter, beat 1 cup plus 2 tablespoons of room temperature butter until fluffy. Peel 3 shallots and 1 garlic clove, chop coarsely and mix thoroughly with 4 large anchovy fillets, 5 tablespoons of parsley and 6 tablespoons of tarragon. Stir the herb mixture into the butter together with 4 tablespoons tomato paste, salt, freshly ground white pepper, and 1 tablespoon cognac. Add more salt, pepper, and cognac to taste.

Côte d'Azur Butter goes well with stuffed poultry, chicken breast, veal chops, and veal medallions.

DELUXE HERB BUTTER

Take $1/4$ teaspoon each freshly chopped marjoram, dill, thyme and rosemary, sweet paprika, curry powder, and cayenne pepper; 3 tablespoons each finely chopped parsley, chives, tarragon; 2 teaspoons mustard and $1^1/2$ teaspoons capers; 1 tablespoon tomato ketchup; 1 oz finely chopped shallots; $2^1/2$ very finely chopped bay leaves; $1/2$ crushed garlic clove; 2 finely chopped anchovy fillets; 1 teaspoon each cognac and Madeira; $1/2$ teaspoon Worcestershire sauce; juice of $1/2$ lemon; a little grated lemon and orange rind, mix thoroughly and leave to marinate at room temperature overnight. Beat 1 cup plus 2 tablespoons of butter until fluffy and work the herb mixture into the butter.

Deluxe Herb Butter is also known as Café de Paris butter. It goes well with loin, rump, and fillet of beef.

GREEN HERB BUTTER

Beat 1 cup plus 2 tablespoons of butter until fluffy. Wash 1 bunch each chives and flat-leafed parsley, chop coarsely, add to boiling, salted water, bring to the boil, drain, refresh in ice-cold water, drain, squeeze out excess moisture, and mix thoroughly with 2 crushed garlic cloves, generous $1/2$ cup finely ground almonds and 2 finely chopped anchovy fillets. Mix into the butter and season to taste with salt, pepper and lemon juice. As alternatives, substitute sorrel or cress for the parsley or chives.

Green Herb Butter is an important accompaniment to fish, and white meat such as poultry and veal.

SALADS AND DRESSINGS

If you like salad, then you will enjoy looking at it as well as eating it. Allow it plenty of room: prepare it in a large serving bowl and serve it on large salad plates.

In Imperial Rome, at the time of the Caesars, it was fashionable to start the meal with a plateful of crispy salad, seasoned with vinegar and salt, and sprinkled with plentiful green herbs. These gourmets called it their "green cake", which accustomed the tongues to delicate flavors and prepared the stomach for the delicacies that would follow. Rome fell, and with it the herb salad. It was one and a half millennia later, in the sixteenth century, that its re-emergence on the tables of the European ruling classes was noted, reputedly introduced by the cooks of Marie de' Medici, the bride of the French king Henri IV. She must surely have known of the letters by the Italian poet Pietro Aretino, who wrote about the salad in which the "acid of the herbs" had to be alleviated "by their sweetness."

"There is a certain amount of learning involved in knowing how to lessen the bitter and acidic taste of some leaves with the neither bitter nor acidic taste of others, to make of the whole such a tender composition that one would wish to eat one's fill. The flowers, which are scattered amongst the delicate green as such pretty and good stimulants to the appetite, bewitch my nose into smelling them, and my hand, to pick them...a handful of unusual herbs, such as wild chicory combined with mint, is worth so much more than lettuce and endive."

There is not much to add to this, and since then salad, in various forms, has remained part of the European menu and become an indispensable element in the American diet. The most interesting development has been the types of salad that became popular in northern regions. It seems that the further north people live, the more they prize sweetness, perhaps as a counterpoint to the harsher climate. For a "sweet" salad, the leaves should be crunchy with freshness, flecked with white from the sour cream or lightly whipped fresh cream, then sprinkled with coarsely chopped herbs, in particular borage, dill, chervil, and chives, and possibly a sprig of parsley, to create the freshest salad you can imagine.

COLORFUL SALADS WITH HERBS

On the one hand what is meant here are the various salad leaves, which harmonize so well with fresh herbs such as salad burnet, borage, and lemon balm; and on the other, salad herbs such as sorrel, cress, and arugula, which combine herb and salad vegetable in one and can be seasoned with other chopped culinary herbs. It does not really matter whether the leaves are classed as salads or herbs, they make a wonderful combination and there is no limit to the mixtures you can create. However, this creative freedom means that there are few definitive recipes for such salads, because they are dependent on what is in season and because it is difficult to give precise quantities, except for the ingredients in the dressing, but even then, personal preference will play a major role.

GREEN SALAD WITH FRESH SHEEP'S-MILK CHEESE

Depending on the quantity, this salad can be served either as an appetizer, or as a filling main course on a warm summer evening. The ingredients in this recipe will serve 1 person.

½ clove garlic
a handful each of seasonal salad leaves (e.g., sorrel. frisée, red-leaf lettuce)
2 cherry tomatoes
a few onion rings
2 tbsp vinaigrette (see pages 88–9)
3 slices fresh sheep's-milk cheese, rolled in chopped parsley
1 nasturtium flower

Dry the washed and cleaned salad leaves. Rub a large wooden salad bowl with the garlic. Put in the lettuces, tomatoes, and onions, add some of the vinaigrette, and toss. Arrange the slices of cheese on a plate, drizzle with a little vinaigrette, arrange the salad on top, and garnish with the nasturtium. Serve with fresh garlic bread, as described on page 93.

Salad dressings

Combining acacia blossom with bitter salad herbs such as dandelion and arugula, and with acidic sorrel emphasizes the powerful, sweet, perfumed taste of these spring blooms.

Whether you prefer a classic vinaigrette, a clear marinade, a heavy mayonnaise or a light yogurt dressing, they are always on the best of terms with fresh herbs and garlic. The simpler the recipe and the fewer ingredients it contains, the more important the quality of those ingredients. This certainly applies to vinaigrette: only the best oil, the best vinegar, and freshly picked herbs will produce a satisfactory result.

VINAIGRETTE

The basic flavor of the vinaigrette depends on the vinegar and oil used. For example, you can use light wine vinegar, spiced vinegar, or fruit-flavored vinegars; strong tasting walnut or hazelnut oil, olive oil, or neutral-tasting sunflower seed or safflower oil. The quality of the mustard will also make a difference to the flavor. As a rule of thumb, use 1 teaspoon mustard to 6–8 tablespoons vinaigrette. Generally speaking, the quantities are based on a ratio of 1 part vinegar to 4 parts oil. If you prefer the fresh acidity of lemon to vinegar, use 1 part lemon juice to 5 parts oil. This classic vinaigrette recipe makes about a $1/2$ cup.

2 tbsp wine vinegar
salt
freshly ground white pepper
1 tsp Dijon mustard
6 tbsp oil

In a bowl, mix together the vinegar with the salt, pepper, and mustard. Gradually add the oil, beating it in with a balloon whisk, until the ingredients combine to form an emulsion.

HERB VINAIGRETTES

Freshly chopped herbs are added to a vinaigrette base. It is up to you to decide which herbs should be combined with which oil, vinegar, or lemon juice, because in the final analysis it depends on what is available in your garden or from the store. The question of which dressing to use with which salad is answered in the following examples.

GREEN SALADS WITH A BITTER FLAVOR

$1/2$ cup vinaigrette made with raspberry vinegar and hazelnut oil
2 tbsp finely chopped shallots
4 tbsp finely chopped herbs (parsley, tarragon, salad burnet, dill, and basil)

LETTUCE-BASED SALADS

$1/2$ cup vinaigrette made with any fruit vinegar
$1/2$ tsp sugar
1 tsp chopped capers
3 tbsp fresh chopped herbs (dill, tarragon, hyssop, and mint)

SALADS WITH COLD OR WARM FISH AND SEAFOOD

$1/2$ cup vinaigrette made with tarragon vinegar
1 tbsp finely chopped onion
2 finely chopped anchovies
2 hard-cooked eggs, chopped
1 tbsp freshly chopped dill
1 tbsp freshly snipped chives
$1/2$ tbsp freshly chopped basil

SALADS WITH MEAT

$1/2$ cup vinaigrette made with red wine vinegar
2 tsp chopped capers
1 small chili pod, deseeded and finely chopped
$1/2$ clove garlic, finely chopped
1 tbsp finely chopped onion
2 tbsp freshly chopped parsley
1 tbsp freshly chopped herbs (chervil, basil, thyme, myrtle)

Preparing a spring salad with fried catfish, this chef uses whatever is available in the store or from the fields — sorrel, dandelion leaves, and especially arugula, which should always be included. Then he adds very thin stalks of raw young asparagus and arranges everything on a plate with 2 small catfish fillets that have been fried until the skin is crisp. He makes a strong salad dressing with pumpkinseed oil and apple vinegar, and seasons it with salt, pepper, plenty of tarragon, and parsley. He then garnishes the salad with acacia blossom.

HERB AND YOGURT DRESSINGS

Yogurt can be used to make fresh, light dressings for green salads, to dress filling salads with pasta, potatoes, fish, or meat. Add the herbs after mixing all the other ingredients together first.

LEMON BALM AND YOGURT DRESSING FOR GREEN SALADS

generous $^1/_3$ cup plain yogurt

2 tbsp orange juice, 2 tsp lemon juice

$^1/_2$ tsp salt, freshly ground white pepper

2 tbsp freshly chopped lemon balm

HERB AND YOGURT DRESSING FOR MEAT OR PASTA SALADS

generous $^1/_3$ cup plain yogurt, $^1/_2$ tbsp balsamic vinegar

$^1/_2$ tsp salt, freshly ground white pepper

$^1/_2$ tbsp chopped capers, 1 tbsp finely chopped shallots

$^1/_2$ clove garlic, finely chopped

1 tbsp chopped celery

2 tbsp freshly chopped herbs (parsley, hyssop, salad burnet, thyme, and rosemary)

A vinaigrette made with red wine vinegar is an excellent complement to a selection of strongly flavored wild salad herbs.

Wild fennel *is a culinary herb with a lot of flavor, usually found on sale only in spring. Both the small bulbs and the green leaves are used.*

SALAD OF LOBSTER, CORN SALAD, AND NASTURTIUMS

2 lobsters, each about 1 1/2 lb
salted water or court bouillon with herbs
For the vinaigrette:
2 tbsp freshly chopped herbs (lemon basil, parsley, salad burnet, tarragon, lovage)
1 tbsp lemon juice, 2 tbsp dry white wine, salt
freshly ground white pepper, 2 tbsp walnut oil, 2 tbsp olive oil
For the salad:
A handful each of corn salad and young nasturtium leaves
8 nasturtium flowers

Boil the lobster in salted water for about 12 minutes. Refresh in ice-cold water, but do not allow to cool completely. To make the vinaigrette, mix the herbs, lemon juice, wine, and seasonings together. Stir into the oils and, if necessary, dilute with chicken stock. Wash the salad leaves, dry, and arrange on 4 plates. Cut the lobster tails into slices with a knife, break off the claws and arrange on the plate of salad. Garnish with nasturtium flowers and pour vinaigrette on top.

MINT SALAD WITH WARM GOAT'S-MILK CHEESE

9 oz goat's-milk cheese, a little flour
1 egg, salt, freshly ground white pepper
a little freshly grated nutmeg, 1 tsp thyme leaves
1 tsp chopped peppermint, 2 tbsp olive oil
1 small oak leaf lettuce, 1 handful fresh peppermint leaves
For the vinaigrette:
2 tbsp finely chopped shallots, 2 tbsp chopped wild fennel
1 clove garlic, finely chopped, a few drops Tabasco sauce
salt, 1 tbsp wine vinegar, 3 tbsp olive oil

Cut the cheese into slices 1/4 in. thick and coat in the flour. Beat the egg and season with salt, pepper, nutmeg, thyme, and mint. Dredge the cheese in the beaten egg mixture and coat in flour again. Heat the oil and fry the cheese slices on both sides until crisp and brown. Mix the shallots, fennel, garlic and seasonings with the vinegar, then stir in the oil.

MESCLUN SALAD WITH PIECES OF WARM CHICKEN

In the south of France it is customary to ask for *un mesclun* if you want a mixed salad, because *mesclun* means mixture.

4 handfuls mixed salad (iceberg lettuce, radicchio, frisée, celery, and parsley leaves)
8 cherry tomatoes
For the vinaigrette:
1 tbsp chopped herbs (chervil, lemon verbena, balm)
1 tsp crushed green peppercorns
1 tbsp chopped scallions, salt
$^1/_4$ tsp sugar, 2 tbsp meat stock
3 tbsp sherry vinegar, 4 tbsp olive oil
For the chicken:
9 oz boned chicken breast
salt, freshly ground white pepper
2 tbsp butter, 1 tbsp veal stock
Optional:
4 quail's eggs, 1 tsp crushed green peppercorns

Wash and dry the salad leaves and cut the tomatoes in half. Mix the herbs, seasonings, and stock with the vinegar, and stir in the oil. Season the chicken breasts and fry on both sides in the hot butter. When cooked, add the veal stock and leave to cool a little. Cut into chunks while still warm. Arrange on plates with the salad and drizzle with vinaigrette. Garnish with a poached quail's egg and sprinkle with the peppercorns.

SALAD OF WILD HERBS WITH FILLET OF RABBIT

In this recipe for herb hunters, use as many different seasonal varieties as possible.

4 handfuls wild herbs (arugula, nettles, dandelion, sorrel or purslane)
For the vinaigrette:
1 chili pod
1 tbsp very finely chopped shallot
$^1/_2$ tsp salt, 1 pinch sugar, 1 tsp thyme
1 tbsp each red wine vinegar and tarragon vinegar
4 tbsp olive oil
For the rabbit pieces:
10 oz boned rabbit pieces
salt, freshly ground white pepper
$4^1/_2$ tsp butter
1 tbsp veal stock
begonia flowers for garnish

Wash and dry the herbs. Deseed the chili pod and slice into thin rings, being careful not to get the juice on your skin or in your eyes. Mix with the shallot, salt, sugar, thyme, and vinegar, then stir in the oil. Season the rabbit and fry in the butter for 3–4 minutes or until tender. Halfway through the cooking time add the veal stock. Leave the rabbit to cool a little in the pan juices. Cut the rabbit into slices while still warm and arrange with the salad. Drizzle with vinaigrette and garnish with flowers.

SOUPS AND SNACKS

Sometimes a mug of soup or a snack is enough to satisfy our appetite. The smaller the portion, the tastier and more nourishing it should be, so be sure to use herbs to enhance these simple, light meals.

The concept of what constitutes soup vegetables differs from country to country. In northern Germany a chunk of celery, a carrot, and celery leaves are tied together with a piece of leek. In France a sprig of thyme, a bay leaf, and any other green herbs that go with the main soup ingredient are added. In eastern Asia the main herb is lemon grass, and in Italy so many herbs are used that you might think they are meant to be the main ingredient themselves. In summer every soup should be flavored with the best the herb garden has to offer. The better ingredients and the greater the care taken with them, the tastier the soup will be. If you grow your own vegetables and herbs, you will want to ensure they are of top quality too. Gardeners know that the purity of the water they use is important to all their growing plants. If you collect rainwater, it should, if possible, be purified in a gravel filter before being used. Herbs alone can make a satisfying snack They should be deliciously sweet or appetizingly sharp, so that all that is needed is a background for them. Because these snacks are all about flavor, great cooks stick to the rule of one herb only, no mixtures.

GARLIC BREAD

In the Mediterranean countries, especially Italy, toasted, seasoned slices of bread are eaten as a snack, as an appetizer, and as an accompaniment to soup. Garlic bread has spread far outside these regional boundaries and become one of the most well-known appetizers. The following recipe is for 1 person.

2–4 slices French bread, depending on size
1 clove garlic, 2 tbsp extra virgin olive oil
salt, freshly ground white pepper

Toast the bread. While it is still hot rub it with the garlic and drizzle with oil. Season with salt and pepper and serve immediately.

There are many variations on this recipe. Try spreading 2 finely chopped garlic cloves and 1 teaspoon chopped parsley on the freshly toasted bread. Drizzle with oil, season with salt, and serve as hot as possible. Instead of parsley you could use other herbs, such as sage, oregano, and thyme.

CREAM OF WATERCRESS SOUP

Oven-fresh garlic bread is an excellent accompaniment to this fresh-tasting herb soup.

2 tbsp butter
$^3/_8$ cup finely chopped shallots
2 cups watercress, stalks removed
$2^1/_4$ cups veal stock
$1^1/_8$ cups light cream
2 egg yolks
$^1/_2$ tsp salt
freshly ground white pepper
$^1/_4$ tsp nutmeg
4 tbsp whipped cream

Melt the butter in a saucepan and soften the shallots and half the watercress in it. Add the veal stock and boil for about 15 minutes. Purée the soup and strain through a sieve. Purée the remaining cress with the light cream in a blender or food processor and add to the stock. Lightly beat the egg yolks and whisk into the soup. Do not allow the soup to boil. Season to taste with salt, pepper, and nutmeg. Finally, carefully fold in the whipped cream. Garnish with cress and serve immediately.

An Italian meal *simply is not complete without antipasti, and there is a huge range, with herbs and garlic playing a major role.*

Delicate morsels

From sautéed olives with herbs to frittered sage leaves, fresh herbs are the simplest way to prepare savory tidbits and snacks.

OLIVE FRITTE

Fried olives are among the most popular antipasti in southern Italy and Greece. They are also enjoyed as a snack with fresh crusty white bread and a glass of wine. In Italy the olives are seasoned with fresh or dried oregano; in Greece the local variety of oregano is used, and usually a sprig of rosemary too.

2⅓ cups black or green olives, 3 cloves garlic
3 tbsp olive oil, 2–3 sprigs oregano
2 tbsp lemon juice, 6 tbsp white wine
coarsely ground white pepper, 1 tsp coarse sea salt

Rinse the olives briefly in warm water and dry carefully. Peel the garlic and slice. Heat the oil in a skillet, sweat the garlic until translucent, add the olives and fry over a reduced heat, turning regularly.

Add half the oregano, pour the lemon juice and white wine on top, season with pepper, and continue to simmer until the liquid is reduced by half. Add the remaining oregano and sprinkle with coarse salt just before serving.

LEAVES AND FLOWERS COOKED IN BATTER

Large leaves and flowers are excellent for dipping in batter and frying. They can be served with a glass of beer or wine, or with soft drinks, at any time of day. Be sure to serve appropriate herbs with your drinks. With non-alcoholic drinks you can serve refreshing, sweet herbs such as peppermint, pineapple sage, and lemon balm. Herbs with a more powerful flavor, such as sage, borage, comfrey, and nasturtium, are more suitable as an accompaniment to wine or beer. Herbs fried in a crisp batter are delicious with a savory dip. Chopped mint and pineapple sage taste particularly good thickly coated in confectioners' sugar.

BASIC RECIPE FOR BATTER

To make the batter light beat the egg white until it stands in soft peaks, and add it separately from the egg yolk.

$^3/_8$ cup flour, $^1/_4$ cup cornstarch
$^1/_2$ tsp salt, 2 tbsp water, 1 egg
oil for frying

Follow the directions given with the illustrations. Heat the oil to 350°F for frying.

INVOLTINI DI SALVIA

This Tuscan speciality is a delicious variation on fried herbs. The savory filling in the sage leaves goes particularly well with a glass of robust Chianti.

24 anchovies
24 big sage leaves, flour, 1 egg
toothpicks, oil for frying

Soak the anchovies in water for 30 minutes so they are not too salty, then leave to drain. Wash the sage leaves under running water, pat dry and roll an anchovy up in each leaf. Secure with a toothpick, dredge in flour, dip in the beaten egg, roll in flour again and fry in the hot oil.

Savory dip. Skin $2^1/_2$ oz tomato and 1 medium red bell pepper. Remove the cores and seeds and purée the flesh to a smooth consistency. Put in a bowl and mix with $^1/_4$ cup finely chopped shallots and 1 finely chopped green chili. Season with $^1/_4$ teaspoon ground chili and $^1/_4$ teaspoon salt. Finally add 2 basil leaves chopped into thin strips.

Preparing and frying batter

Beat the flour, cornstarch, salt, water, and egg yolk together with a balloon whisk to form a smooth batter. Fold in the egg white last.

Grasp the washed and thoroughly dried leaves or flowers by the stems and carefully dip them in the batter.

Fry in the oil until crisp and golden. Remove and leave to drain on paper towels.

SMOKED SALMON WITH DILL SAUCE AND POTATO PANCAKES

2$^1/_2$ oz smoked salmon
For the potato pancakes:
2 medium-sized potatoes, 2 eggs, 8 tsp light cream, 4 tsp milk
salt, freshly grated nutmeg, 2 tbsp butter
For the dill sauce:
1$^1/_8$ cups fish stock, 2 shallots
generous $^1/_2$ cup crème fraîche, juice of $^1/_2$ lemon
salt, cayenne pepper, 2 tbsp chopped dill

Finely dice the salmon. To make the pancakes, peel the potatoes, cut into quarters, and cook in boiling salted water. While still hot, purée them, mix with the eggs, cream, and milk, and season with salt and nutmeg. Leave to rest for 1 hour. Preheat the oven to 400°F. Heat the butter in a frying pan, add about 1 tablespoon potato batter per pancake and, using a spoon, spread to form pancakes about 2 in. in diameter. Place them in the oven and bake until golden brown, turning occasionally. To make the dill sauce, reduce the fish stock by half. Peel the shallots, chop finely, blanch briefly, leave to drain, then add to the reduced stock. Stir in the crème fraîche and season with lemon juice, salt and cayenne pepper. Finally, add the chopped dill. Put the dill sauce on a warmed plate, arrange the salmon and pancakes on top and garnish with sprigs of dill.

CHICKEN WITH MUSHROOM AND HERBS

2 boned chicken breasts, skinless
salt, freshly ground white pepper
juice of 1 lemon, 1 tsp mustard
4 tsp each chopped parsley and tarragon
4 button mushrooms, watercress
2 tbsp butter
For the parsley vinaigrette:
$^1/_4$ cup champagne vinegar, salt
freshly ground white pepper, 1$^3/_8$ cups vegetable oil
$^1/_4$ cup puréed parsley (see page 78)

Cut each chicken breast in half horizontally and trim the end to make evenly shaped pieces. Season them with salt and pepper, drizzle with a little lemon juice, spread thinly with mustard and season with the herbs. Clean the mushrooms and slice very thinly. Arrange the mushrooms and watercress in overlapping layers on the pieces of chicken, pressing lightly into the layer of mustard and herbs. Heat the butter in a frying pan and sauté the chicken pieces gently until done, drizzling the tops of the chicken with the butter from time to time. When cooked, place under a medium broiler until the tops are crisp. To make the vinaigrette, mix all the ingredients together. Place the chicken on a plate, garnish with watercress and radishes, and coat in the vinaigrette.

CRISPY SALMON ON A BED OF WATERCRESS PURÉE

8 pieces salmon fillet, about 1¹/₂ in. sq. with skin, salt
For the watercress purée:
2¹/₄ lb watercress
6 shallots, 1 small onion
2 tbsp butter, 1¹/₈ cup chicken stock
salt, freshly ground white pepper
For the red wine sauce:
1 shallot, 2 tsp red wine, 4 tbsp chilled, diced butter
For the garnish:
16 nasturtium leaves, nasturtium flowers

Cut a lattice pattern into the skin side of the salmon squares, season with salt and fry in a pan without fat. for 3–5 minutes. In the meantime carefully wash the watercress, blanch, refresh in ice-cold water, and squeeze well to remove excess liquid. Peel the shallots and the onion, and finely dice. Melt the butter in a saucepan, add the onion and shallot, and soften very slightly. Add the watercress and chicken stock, and simmer gently for 10 minutes. Purée in a food processor, and season with salt and pepper. To make the red wine sauce, finely chop the shallot, put into a saucepan with the red wine, and boil until reduced to about one-third. To thicken, add the chilled butter, and whisk. Arrange the nasturtium leaves and flowers on plates, spoon 2 tablespoons watercress purée on to each plate, place 2 salmon squares on top of the purée and garnish with 1 tablespoon of red wine sauce.

POTATO SOUFFLÉ ON A BED OF FLAT-LEAF PARSLEY

For the potato soufflé:
4 floury potatoes, 4 egg yolks, 4 tbsp farmer's cheese
³/₄ cup light cream, 8 egg whites, salt, freshly grated nutmeg
For the parsley bed:
1 bunch flat-leaf parsley, 2 scallions
3 cups chanterelle mushrooms, 1 tbsp butter
16 slices smoked bacon
For the vinaigrette:
1 tsp balsamic vinegar
salt, freshly ground white pepper, 4 tbsp olive oil

Boil the potatoes in their skins, peel them, and mash. Carefully fold in the egg yolks, the drained curd cheese, and the cream. Stiffly beat the egg whites and fold into the mixture. Season to taste with salt and nutmeg. Fill 4 buttered ramekins to about ³/₄ in. below the top with potato mixture. Place them in a hot bain-marie (the water should come two-thirds of the way up the dishes) and cook for 12–15 minutes in an oven preheated to 350°F. Strip the parsley leaves from the stalks. Finely dice the scallions. Fry the chanterelles in butter. Fry the bacon until crisp. To make the vinaigrette, mix together vinegar, salt, and pepper, and stir in the oil. Arrange the parsley and scallions on 4 plates, drizzle with vinaigrette, arrange chanterelles and 4 strips of bacon on top. Turn out the soufflés onto the salad and serve immediately.

Chervil, bear's garlic, and sorrel

These are traditional herbs for use in soup, which taste best with plenty of cream, but why not try experimenting with other herbs too? Anise hyssop or lemon basil, for example, lend a very distinctive flavor to a creamy soup.

CREAM OF CHERVIL SOUP WITH CHICKEN AND COMFREY

A typical spring soup, as this is the time when chervil and comfrey develop the best flavor.

1 handful fresh chervil
1 potato
4^1/$_2$ cups chicken stock
salt, ^{1}/$_2$ tsp freshly ground white pepper
freshly ground nutmeg
^{7}/$_8$ cup light cream
2 tbsp butter
2 slices white bread, crusts removed
6 oz boned chicken
2 comfrey leaves
^{1}/$_4$ cup whipped cream
1 tbsp chervil leaves, to garnish

Wash the chervil, pat dry, and remove leaves from stems. Put the stems to one side and chop the leaves. Peel the potato and dice finely. Heat the stock, add the chervil stems and diced potato, and simmer for 20 minutes. Purée the mixture in a food processor and, if required, strain through a sieve. Pour into a saucepan, add the chopped chervil leaves and bring to the boil again. Season heavily with salt, pepper, and nutmeg. Add the light cream and bring the soup to the boil, stirring constantly. Remove from heat to prevent further boiling, which would impair the delicate flavor. Heat the butter in a skillet, cut the bread into cubes, and fry until crisp and golden. Cut the chicken into small cubes, add to the pan, and fry gently until cooked. Finally, cut the comfrey leaves into strips, and add to the pan. Quickly stir the whipped cream into the soup, garnish with the chicken, croûtons, and chervil leaves, and serve immediately.

Fine cooking deserves
a fine wine to
accompany it. When
making regional dishes,
drink regional wines to
appreciate the authentic
taste.

CREAM OF BEAR'S GARLIC SOUP WITH CHAR AND WILD ASPARAGUS

A combination of powerful contrasts — strong-flavored bear's garlic soup and delicate char fillets.

For the cream of bear's garlic soup:
1 handful crushed bear's garlic leaves
9 cups salted water, $4^1/_2$ cups fish or veal stock
2–3 tbsp dry white wine
$^1/_2$ tsp salt, freshly ground white pepper
3 tbsp butter, diced and chilled
dash light cream, optional
For the garnish:
$^1/_2$ tsp coriander seeds, 2 char fillets
salt, freshly ground white pepper
2 tsp lime juice
8 small asparagus spears (wild asparagus if possible)
3 tbsp butter for frying
grated sautéed celeriac

Wash the bear's garlic, remove the stems, and blanch the leaves briefly in boiling salted water. Pat dry and purée in a food processor (if necessary, add a little stock). Bring the bear's garlic purée to the boil with the stock and the wine, season with salt and pepper. Stir the chilled, diced butter into the soup to enrich it, and add a dash of cream if liked. To make the garnish, coarsely crush the coriander seeds and fry in a pan without fat. Season the char fillets on both sides with salt, pepper, and coriander, and drizzle with lime juice. Shape the fillets into a loop and fry in the hot butter with the cleaned asparagus. Arrange the char fillets and the asparagus in the middle of the soup plate and pour in the bear's garlic soup. Garnish with grated sautéed celeriac.

CREAM OF SORREL SOUP

A genuine spring soup, for which the powerful taste of wild sorrel is best. Substitute watercress for a more delicate variation.

4 cups sorrel
$^1/_2$ unpeeled garlic clove
2 tbsp butter
3 slices stale white bread, crusts removed
$4^1/_2$ cups veal stock, 1 tbsp white vermouth
$^7/_8$ cup light cream
salt, freshly ground white pepper
scant $^1/_2$ cup whipped cream

Wash the sorrel, pat dry and remove leaves from stems. Melt the butter in a large saucepan. Crush the garlic clove and sweat it in the butter. Cut the white bread into cubes, add to the pan, and fry until crisp and golden. Remove and drain on paper towels. Add the stock, the white vermouth, the light cream, and then the sorrel leaves to the pan and boil until the liquid is reduced to one-third. Pour into a food processor, purée, and strain through a sieve into a saucepan. Season with salt and pepper, and heat. Fold in the whipped cream, heat again, and serve. Serve the croûtons separately.

The quality of a soup begins with a good basic stock. Of course, only the best, freshest ingredients, whether meat or herbs, will do.

With or without garnish

Both the soup itself and the garnish can be seasoned with herbs, as shown in the three examples here.

TWO-COLOR PARSLEY SOUP

This recipe is an interplay between color and taste.

1$^1/_4$ lb turnip-rooted parsley (Hamburg parsley)
4 tbsp butter
4$^1/_2$ cups chicken stock
$^7/_8$ cup light cream
5$^1/_4$ cups flat-leaf parsley

Wash the parsley root, peel, and cut into small pieces. Heat the butter in a large pot, add the parsley root and fry gently. Pour in the chicken stock and simmer until the parsley root is soft. Pour in the cream and stir. Purée the soup in a blender or food processor, then strain through a sieve. Put half of the soup to one side. Blanch the flat-leaf parsley, refresh in ice-cold water, squeeze well to remove moisture, and chop very finely.

Stir the parsley purée into half of the soup so it takes on an attractive green color. Heat up the white and green soups separately, then pour both into a soup plate simultaneously. They will not run into each other because they both have the same consistency.

CONSOMMÉ WITH HERB TERRINE

Here is a tasty terrine made with chicken livers and spinach, flavored with herbs, to serve with consommé.

4$^1/_2$ cups beef consommé
For the chicken liver stuffing:
$^1/_4$ cup finely chopped onions
2 tbsp butter
6 oz (1$^1/_4$ cups) chicken livers
$^1/_2$ bunch finely chopped parsley, 1 sprig marjoram
salt, freshly ground white pepper
For the spinach stuffing:
7 cups fresh spinach
2 tbsp each finely chopped parsley and chervil
2 tbsp ricotta cheese
salt, freshly ground white pepper
freshly grated nutmeg
Additional:
2 thin slices bread
2 tbsp butter for frying

To make the chicken liver stuffing, sweat the onions in the butter until soft. Add the chicken livers, increase the heat, and cook for 3–4 minutes. Mix in the herbs and seasoning. Place livers and any pan juices in a mortar and pound to a purée with the pestle. Press the purée through a sieve. To make the spinach stuffing, clean the leaves and remove the stems. Place in a saucepan with 1 tablespoon of water and cook. Squeeze all moisture out of the cooked leaves and chop. Place in a bowl with the cheese, herbs, and seasoning, and mix. Cut the slices of bread in half. Spread each half with chicken liver purée on one side and spinach on the other. Sandwich two halves together so that the layers of chicken liver and spinach are next to each other. Heat the butter in a skillet until foaming, place the slices in the pan and then bake in an oven preheated to 350°F until both sides have acquired a good color. Cut into slices, arrange on plates, and pour the hot consommé on top.

CREAM OF HERB SOUP WITH SWEETBREADS AND CHANTERELLE MUSHROOMS

This soup is given a velvety consistency by gently cooking cream with the stock and then adding whipped cream.

4 cups herbs (chervil, tarragon, sorrel, chives)
1¼ cups strong chicken stock
salt, pepper, nutmeg, ⁷⁄₈ cup light cream
4 tbsp chilled butter, scant ½ cup whipped cream
9 oz veal sweetbreads, 1 tsp vegetable oil
2 tsp butter
2 cups cleaned chanterelle mushrooms, salt

Wash and dry the herbs. Strip the leaves from the chervil and tarragon, remove the stems from the sorrel, and purée in a blender with the chives and a little stock. Bring the remaining stock to the boil and season well. Pour the light cream into the boiling stock, stirring all the time, and cook gently. Add the herb purée and simmer gently for 1–2 minutes. Enrich the the creamy soup with the chilled butter and, finally, fold in the whipped cream. Divide the sweetbreads into 12 pieces and fry in the oil until brown all over. Add half the butter to the oil, heat until foaming and coat the sweetbreads in the butter. Heat the remaining butter in another pan, fry the chanterelles in the butter and season to taste. Arrange the sweetbreads and chanterelles in soup plates and pour the soup on top.

EGGS AND CHEESE

Eggs and cheese are culinary brothers and sisters. The ability of one to bind and the creamy, melting quality of the other can be combined in innumerable ways.

The addition of the right herb can turn a simple dish into a culinary masterpiece, to the delight of cooks and gourmets alike. Eggs and herbs are the stars of quick and easy cooking, the professional's cuisine, for people who have neither the time nor the energy to prepare complex meals at the end of the day. An omelet or scrambled eggs with herbs makes a filling and satisfying meal. The addition of cheese to this combination, and the pairing of cheese and herbs alone have also been honored since time immemorial. Not only do herbs go well with any kind of cheese, they are also good for the cows and goats to eat: there is no better milk than that from cows that have fed on wild herbs.

SCRAMBLED EGGS WITH PARSLEY, BUTTON MUSHROOMS, AND HERBS

A delicate combination of ingredients that suit each other perfectly.

For the mushrooms:
6 cups cleaned button mushrooms, 2 tbsp butter
$1/2$ tsp salt, freshly ground white pepper
2 tbsp chopped parsley
1 tbsp chopped mixed herbs (chives, basil, hyssop, and thyme)
For the scrambled eggs:
8 eggs, 4 tbsp light cream
1 tsp salt, freshly ground white pepper
1 tbsp chopped parsley, 2 tbsp butter

Clean and slice the mushrooms. Heat the butter in a skillet and fry the mushrooms for 4–5 minutes. Season with salt and pepper, and mix with the finely chopped herbs. Remove from the pan and keep warm. To make the scrambled eggs, break the eggs into a bowl and mix well with the cream, salt, pepper, and parsley. Heat the butter in a skillet and pour in the egg mixture. As soon as the egg begins to set, stir and draw into the middle of the pan until it is evenly cooked and creamy, yet still moist. If you prefer, the eggs can be allowed to set into an omelette. Mix the warm mushrooms with the scrambled egg, or use to fill the omelet. Serve immediately. Goes well with fresh crusty white bread and salad.

SCRAMBLED EGGS WITH PARSLEY, WARM FILLET OF SMOKED HERRING, AND HERBS

In this recipe the smoky taste of the fish goes well with the eggs and herbs.

2 smoked herrings, $4^1/2$ tsp butter
1 handful herbs (parsley, basil and thyme)
1 turnip-rooted parsley (Hamburg parsley), oil for frying
1 recipe scrambled eggs with parsley (see left)

Carefully bone the herring and fry in the butter. Sprinkle the freshly chopped herbs over the fish and turn the fish in the herbs to coat. To make the parsley chips, clean the turnip-rooted parsley, cut into wafer-thin slices, and fry in the hot oil until crisp and brown. Arrange the fish fillets on a plate with the parsley chips and serve with the scrambled eggs.

HERB CHEESE SOUFFLÉ

There is no lighter and airier way of enjoying herbs and cheese! If you follow the sequence of illustrations opposite, you can be confident that your soufflé will rise. Herbs, eggs, and cheese are folded into a béchamel sauce and baked together. As with all mixtures that include egg white to help the recipe rise, you must choose the right moment to fold the extremely delicate egg white into the herb and cheese sauce, and do it in such a way that as much volume as possible is retained. The best way is to fold the eggs into the mixture as soon as they form stiff peaks and are glossy.

4 tbsp butter
1/4 cup flour
1 1/8 cups milk
1/2 tsp salt, freshly ground white pepper
a little grated nutmeg
4 tbsp light cream
5 egg yolks
2 tbsp each chopped parsley and chives
1 1/2 tsp each chopped thyme and marjoram
1 1/4 cups shredded mature Swiss Gruyère cheese
5 egg whites, stiffly beaten
butter for greasing the dish

Prepare the cheese and herb soufflé as described on the right. You need a 5-cup capacity soufflé dish for the stated quantities. The soufflé is baked on a low shelf at 350°F for 20 minutes, then at 400°F for 20–25 minutes. It is done when it is a rich brown color and has risen well.

How to prepare a cheese and herb soufflé

Melt the butter in a saucepan, then add the flour all at once.

Reduce the heat and stir vigorously with a balloon whisk for 2–3 minutes.

Gradually stir in the milk. Season, bring to the boil and simmer for 5 minutes.

Keep stirring right around the bottom of the saucepan to prevent sticking. Add the cream. Remove from heat.

Stir in the egg yolks one at a time. The next egg should be added only when the previous one has been blended in completely.

Add the herbs and cheese. Transfer the mixture to a mixing bowl and leave to cool a little.

Using a spatula, fold the stiffly beaten egg whites into the warm herb and cheese mixture.

Pour the prepared mixture into a buttered soufflé dish and place immediately in a preheated oven.

OMELET WITH BASIL AND GOAT'S-MILK CHEESE

The goat's-milk cheese should be quite ripe and runny to give the omelet a piquant flavor. Other strong cheeses, such as blue cheese, Appenzell, and Camembert can also be used; they should then be combined with strong-flavored herbs such as thyme or lovage. This recipe serves 1 person.

2 eggs
$1/4$ tsp salt, freshly ground white pepper
3 oz goat's-milk cheese
1 tbsp coarsely chopped basil
2 tbsp butter

Break the eggs into a bowl, season with salt and pepper and beat well. Cut the goat's-milk cheese into cubes and stir into the eggs with the basil. Heat the butter in a frying pan, pour in the egg mixture and reduce the heat a little. Allow the omelet to set slowly, turn if necessary and cook other side. Serve with a fresh green salad.

SHEEP'S-MILK CHEESE IN OLIVE OIL WITH HERBS

When combined with a strong-flavored olive oil, the herbs bring out the full taste of the sheep's-milk cheese and improve its keeping qualities.

4 fresh sheep's-milk cheeses, 4 oz each
$1/2$ tsp black peppercorns
$1/2$ tsp white peppercorns
$1/2$ tsp coriander seeds
2 sprigs thyme
4 bay leaves
4 stems fennel
2 sprigs rosemary
2 sprigs summer savory
$4^1/2$ – 9 cups olive oil

Layer the sheep's-milk cheese, spices, and herbs in a sealable glass jar and fill with olive oil to cover. Seal the jar and leave the cheese to marinate in the oil for 3–4 weeks so that it is infused with the flavor of the spices and herbs.

Preserving them with herbs in oil enhances the flavor of both sheep's-milk and goat's-milk cheese.

Savory baking with herbs

Herbs are an ideal seasoning for quiches, and the scent of oregano immediately identifies a freshly baked pizza.

SMALL HERB QUICHE

Aromatic marjoram with basil and sharp summer savory make these quiches taste especially good. This recipe makes 8 quiches, each $4\frac{1}{2}$ in. in diameter.

For the pastry:
$1\frac{1}{2}$ cups wholewheat flour
7 tbsp butter, cubed
$\frac{1}{4}$ tsp salt
4 tbsp water
For the filling:
$\frac{1}{2}$ lb unsliced smoked bacon
$1\frac{1}{4}$ cups freshly shredded Swiss cheese
4 eggs
$\frac{1}{4}$ tsp salt
freshly ground pepper
4 tbsp chopped herbs (marjoram, basil, summer savory)
$1\frac{1}{8}$ cups light cream

To make the pastry, rub the butter into the flour and salt by hand or in a food processor to produce a crumbly texture. Add the water and mix well. Leave to rest in the refrigerator for 1 hour. Roll out the pastry to $\frac{1}{8}$ in. thick, and use to line the pans, pressing down well around the edges. There is no need to grease the pans first. Prepare the filling as illustrated and use to fill the pastry cases.

Sicilian Sfincione pizza is distinguished by the incomparable flavor of the oregano that flourishes in the mountains of Sicily. This crispy "peasant food", traditionally baked in an old stone oven, can be flavored with innumerable toppings and seasonings, although the basic ingredients are always the same.

How to make quiche filling
Cut the smoked bacon into small cubes and add to a bowl with the eggs and cheese.

Season, add the chopped herbs, and stir to distribute evenly, then add the cream.

Mix all the ingredients together briefly with a balloon whisk, but do not beat the egg mixture, or the herb juices will turn the mixture green.

Pour into the pastry cases, smooth the top, and bake in a preheated oven at 400°F for 20–25 minutes until golden brown.

BASIC RECIPE FOR PIZZA DOUGH

This recipe is sufficient for 2 pizzas, each 12 in. in diameter.

2¹/₂ cups all-purpose flour, 2 tbsp yeast
¹/₂ cup lukewarm water
¹/₂ tsp salt
2 tbsp olive oil

Put the flour into a bowl and make a well in the center. Dissolve the yeast in lukewarm water, pour into the flour well and sprinkle a little flour on top. Cover the bowl with a cloth and leave the yeast mixture to work in a warm place until cracks appear on the surface. Add the salt and oil, and stir in. Turn the ingredients out on to a floured counter and knead to make a smooth dough. Cover and leave to rise again. For each pizza, roll out the dough to a circle or rectangle with the edge a little thicker than the rest. Place on a lightly greased baking sheet. Prick the surface several times with a fork and cover with topping. Simple pizzas, with perhaps two or three toppings, taste especially good. Place the prepared pizzas in a preheated oven at 425°F for about 25 minutes until crisp and brown.

PIZZA AGLIO E OLIO

Garlic is the dominant flavor in this pizza. Make two pizzas, each 12 in. in diameter, using the basic recipe above. Spread at least 4 chopped cloves of garlic over the pizza, season with salt and pepper, sprinkle a pinch of rubbed oregano on top if liked, and drizzle with plenty of olive oil. Bake as above.

PIZZA MARGHERITA

This famous combination of tomatoes, cheese, and basil is simple, but stylish. Make the pizza according to the basic recipe above. Skin, deseed, and chop 1³/₄ lb tomatoes, and spread on the pizza base. Top with ¹/₂ lb mozzarella cheese and 1 cup chopped fresh basil, salt, and pepper. Drizzle with lots of olive oil and bake as above.

PASTA, RICE, AND POTATOES

These are the stalwarts of the kitchen. If you have them in the house and a supply of herbs, you will always be able to prepare a tasty meal quickly.

There are islands in the Mediterranean that can be smelled from afar. The sun shines down on the bushes of rosemary and carpet of wild thyme, and the breeze wafts the scent over the sea. Because the herbs here do not have to struggle to reach the sun, all their energy goes into producing flavor and aroma. While the sun shines, the essential oils are concentrated in the small, tender leaves as they unfold. In the Middle Ages Venice was one of the most important centers for handling as yet unknown vegetables and herbs from the Middle and Far East. So that the seeds and roots of these plants did not die, they were given a temporary home in the city gardens, growing in the shade of tall, ivy-clad walls, where they could be inspected and bought. People at that time would have compared the differences in herbs when cooked, how the green color of some faded when used in a stock, how strong others were, how they helped to stimulate the appetite. The entire Mediterranean region became an ideal testing ground for all kinds of herbs because of the warm climate and the preference for light food. Quickly cooked, neutral tasting pasta and rice were ideal partners for the finest herbs then, as they are now, with the picture completed by olive oil or butter. Add a sprig of a fresh, sun-drenched herb to melted butter in a pan, and toss cooked spaghetti in it for a simple and simply delicious dish. Potatoes too are nothing more than a floury base for coatings and flavorings, and in any form they make a perfect match with herbs. Try them dusted with flour and boiled with shallots or celery hearts, anchovies, and parsley; with dill and cream; with a mixture of basil, parsley, and tarragon; with peppermint; or simply buttered and sprinkled with chives.

TAGLIATELLE WITH TOMATO AND HERB SAUCE

The combination of garlic, fresh herbs, and tomatoes is not only typically Italian, but also simply the best thing you can serve with pasta. It is very simple to prepare if the tomatoes are ripe and the herbs come straight from the garden or market.

14 oz tagliatelle or fettucine
salted water, 3 tbsp good quality olive oil
$^{3}/_{8}$ cup finely chopped onion
2 cloves garlic, finely chopped
$^{1}/_{2}$ lb tomatoes, 2 anchovies
2 tbsp dry white wine
$^{1}/_{2}$ tsp salt, freshly ground white pepper
3 tbsp chopped herbs (parsley, basil, oregano, sage, and thyme)
$^{3}/_{4}$ cup grated Parmesan cheese

Cook the pasta in boiling, salted water until *al dente*, pour off water and leave the pasta in a sieve to drain. Heat the oil in a large skillet, add the onions and garlic , and fry until transparent. Blanch the tomatoes briefly, remove skins, cut in half and remove seeds. Cut the flesh into cubes and add to the onions with the chopped anchovies. Add the wine and sweat for about 5 minutes; season with salt and pepper. Add the chopped herbs and sweat for a further 5 minutes. Carefully stir the pasta into the sauce and heat through. Sprinkle with the grated cheese, stir in lightly and serve.

This basic recipe can be varied with different ingredients. For Spaghetti alla Vongole use spaghetti instead of ribbon pasta and increase the quantity of white wine to $^{1}/_{2}$ cup. Cook $1^{1}/_{4}$ lb of fresh clams in the sauce until they open.

Herbs in wafer-thin pasta

Here is an attractive and tasty way to serve pasta. Try out new patterns with different herbs, because each one has its own unique flavor. The method is very simple. Position the herbs between sheets of thin pasta dough, then roll out the combined layers as thinly as possible. The herbs take on unusual, skeletal shapes. You can use either a pasta machine or a rolling pin, although the latter requires more effort. Using the machine, first roll out a strip of dough about $^1/_{32}$ in. thick, arrange the herbs on top and cover with another strip of dough. The dough must be absolutely fresh, otherwise the herbs will not stick to it. If the dough begins to dry out, spray lightly with water immediately. Pass the dough filled with herbs through the machine again to the same thickness. Because the strips of dough are rolled only in one direction, they and their contents are stretched out to twice the length, which creates the patterns.

BASIC RECIPE FOR PASTA DOUGH
The quality of the flour determines the consistency of the dough. Flour made from durum wheat is best.

2 cups all-purpose flour
2 eggs, 1 egg yolk
$^1/_2$ tsp salt

Prepare the dough as described in the sequence of illustrations. Herb pasta, especially that which contains chopped herbs, can be cut into different shapes and sizes. Large squares or rectangles are the best way to display these herb patterns.

QUADRUCCI IN BRODO
In Italy the herb pasta is served in a clear chicken or beef broth.

16–20 pasta squares with herbs
1 small carrot
1–1$^1/_2$ stalks celery
4$^1/_2$ cups meat broth
1 tbsp chopped herbs (parsley and chives)

Cook the pasta in boiling water until done, drain, and reserve. Meanwhile cut the carrots into matchsticks and the celery into small pieces. Cook until just tender in about 1 cup of broth. Add the remaining broth, bring to the boil, and add the pasta. Heat slowly and serve sprinkled with the chopped herbs.

How to prepare and decorate pasta dough
Sieve the flour on to a counter and make a well in the center. Put the eggs, egg yolks, and salt in the well. Working from the center outwards, mix the ingredients until all the flour is incorporated. Knead the dough until it is smooth and elastic, adding more flour or water if necessary. Wrap in plastic wrap and leave to rest for 1 hour.

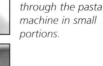

Roll the dough through the pasta machine in small portions.

Arrange as many herbs as possible on the strip of dough, place another strip on top, and press down firmly.

Pass the filled strips of dough through the rollers again. The sheets of dough will increase to twice the length.

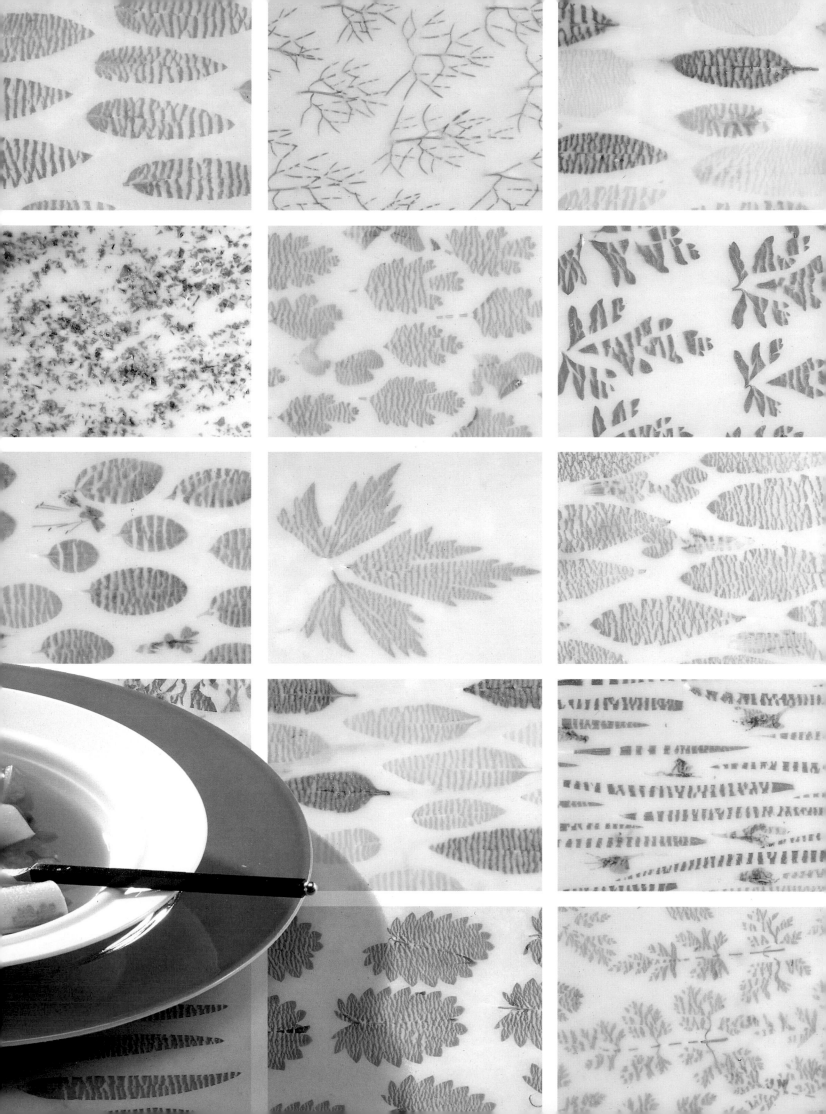

GNOCCHI WITH WILD HERBS

1³/₄ lb mixed salad herbs (dandelion, nettle, sorrel, chicory, fennel)
generous 1¹/₄ cups ricotta cheese, 1 cup freshly grated pecorino cheese
1 egg, 1 cup freshly grated Parmesan cheese
¹/₂ tsp salt, freshly ground white pepper
freshly grated nutmeg, 1 cup all-pupose flour
7 tbsp butter, 2 oz thinly sliced Parmesan cheese

Cook the herbs in a large saucepan with a little water until soft. Drain and leave to dry. Chop finely and put into a bowl. Mix in the ricotta, pecorino, egg, and grated Parmesan cheese. Season with salt, pepper, and nutmeg. Dust hands with flour and make little egg-shaped dumplings about 1¹/₄ in. in diameter from the mixture and turn them gently in flour. Bring salted water to the boil in a large saucepan. Put small quantities of the dumplings into the water. As soon as they rise to the surface, remove them with a slotted spoon, drain and keep warm, repeating the process until all the gnocchi are cooked. Melt the butter in a small saucepan. Sprinkle the gnocchi with the thin slices of Parmesan and drizzle the melted butter on top, then serve immediately.

HERB-FILLED RAVIOLI

Pansoti is the name for these special ravioli in Liguria. They are made in spring and filled with the local wild herbs: dandelion, sorrel, borage, chervil, wild chicory and fennel, as well as the delicate wild onion, rocambole.

For the filling:
9 oz fresh, mixed wild herbs, 9 oz young spinach
generous 1¹/₄ cups ricotta cheese, ³/₄ cup grated Parmesan cheese
1 egg, 1 tbsp finely chopped shallots
1 clove garlic, finely chopped
¹/₂ tsp salt, freshly ground white pepper
For the sauce:
2¹/₄ cups walnuts, 2 slices stale white bread
scant ¹/₂ cup milk, ¹/₂ tsp salt, 1 clove garlic, chopped
4 tbsp good quality olive oil, generous ¹/₄ cup grated Parmesan cheese
4 tbsp yogurt, 6 tbsp milk
For the pasta dough:
3¹/₂ cups flour, 1 egg, 1 tsp vinegar, 6–8 tbsp water
For the garnish:
4 tbsp butter, 1 tbsp chopped wild herbs
grated Parmesan cheese

To make the filling, blanch the herbs and spinach, and squeeze to remove moisture. Process in a blender or food processor to a soft green paste. Stir in the cheeses, egg, shallots, and garlic, and season with salt and pepper. To make the sauce, blanch the nuts briefly in boiling water and remove the skins. Soften the bread in the milk and press out the liquid. Process the nuts, bread, salt, and garlic in a food processor, and pass through a medium-meshed sieve if necessary. Gradually add the olive oil and stir into the mixture thoroughly. Add the Parmesan cheese, and finally stir

in the yogurt and milk. To make the dough, sieve the flour on to a counter and make a well in the center. Add the egg, vinegar, and half the water and knead to form a smooth dough. If necessary, add the remaining water. Cover and leave to rest for 1 hour. Roll out thinly and cut into 2-in. squares. Divide the filling among half the squares. Dampen the edges of the squares with water, place an unfilled pasta square on top of each and press the edges down firmly so that the filling will not escape during cooking. Cook in boiling, salted water for 4–5 minutes, drain, and arrange on plates. Gently brown the butter, add the chopped herbs, and drizzle over the pasta. Serve with the walnut sauce and grated Parmesan cheese.

HERB RAVIOLI ON A BED OF PARSLEY SAUCE WITH SAUTÉED MUSHROOMS

This simple vegetarian dish is best prepared in advance and frozen.

For the pasta dough:
7 cups flour, 3¹/₂ cups durum wheat semolina
15 egg yolks, 2 tbsp olive oil
pinch salt, egg yolk for glazing
For the herb filling:
1 bunch each chervil and parsley, small bunch chives
1¹/₄ cup soft mashed potato, made with 4 tbsp butter
fried croûtons made from 1 thin slice bread
For the parsley sauce:
3 bunches parsley, 1 cup chicken stock,
¹/₂ cup Champagne
2 tsp chilled butter, ¹/₂ tbsp whipped cream
For the mushrooms:
3 cups mushrooms, 1–2 tbsp olive oil
squeeze lemon juice, salt
¹/₂ clove garlic

Knead together all the ingredients for the pasta dough, except the egg yolk for glazing. Shape into a ball, wrap in plastic wrap, and chill for 2–3 hours. Prepare the filling. Chop the herbs quite finely, mix with the mashed potato and the croûtons. Roll out the pasta dough on a floured counter to form a long rectangle. Draw a line across the middle of the dough and brush one half with the egg yolk. Place little heaps of filling on the dough 2 in. apart and cover with the other half of the dough. Using a smooth or fluted cutter, cut out circles 2 in. in diameter. Using a slightly smaller cutter, press the edges together so the filling does not escape during cooking. Place in boiling, salted water and cook for 3–4 minutes. To make the sauce, blanch the parsley, purée in a mixer, and pass through a sieve. Reduce the chicken stock to half the quantity, add the champagne, and bring to the boil again. Whisk the parsley into the sauce, add the chilled butter, and whisk again, and then fold in the whipped cream. Pour immediately on to a warmed plate and place a ravioli parcel on top. While the stock is reducing clean the mushrooms, cut large stalks and caps into slices, and leave small caps whole. Fry in olive oil, season to taste with lemon juice, salt and garlic and arrange around the ravioli.

Risotto with herbs

Herbs make a perfect seasoning for risotto, either on their own or in a mixture, as the recipes on these pages show. If the rissoto is to be strongly flavored with herbs and colored with the juices, then the herbs should go into the pan immediately after the rice. If the flavor should be delicate and restrained, then the herbs are added after cooking, but before the risotto is seasoned with salt and pepper.

RISOTTO WITH WILD HERBS

This risotto tastes best in spring when nettles, dandelion and bear's garlic are still young and tender. The herbs need not be blanched first. The risotto takes on a special flavor from the delicate rocambole (wild onion) but if it is unavailable, scallions can be used instead.

4 tbsp good quality vegetable oil
$1/2$ cup finely chopped rocambole, with green
1 clove garlic, finely chopped
3 cups young spinach
3 cups wild herbs (nettle, dandelion, bear's garlic)
2 tbsp white wine
2 cups arborio rice, $6^{1}/4$ cups warm veal stock
$1/2$ tsp salt, freshly ground white pepper
1 cup freshly grated Parmesan cheese, 3 tbsp butter

Heat the oil in a large saucepan, fry the rocambole and garlic until transparent. Add the washed and chopped spinach, and herbs, pour in the white wine and simmer together for 1–2 minutes. Add the rice and fry until transparent. Pour in half of the veal stock and cook on a medium heat, uncovered, until the rice has absorbed all the liquid. Gradually add the rest of the stock, and cook until it has all been absorbed and the rice is soft. Season with salt and pepper. Sprinkle with the grated cheese, dot with butter, and cover the pan. Leave to marinate for a few minutes until the butter has melted. Remove the lid, stir the risotto, and serve.

RISOTTO WITH BASIL

This is a good example of a fine risotto flavored with one herb and garlic, which goes superbly with the basil.

2 tbsp olive oil
1^1/$_2$ tbsp beef marrow
^{3}/$_8$ cup chopped shallots
2 cloves garlic, crushed
2 cups arborio rice
^{1}/$_2$ cup dry white wine
6^1/$_4$ cups warm chicken stock
^{1}/$_2$ tsp salt
freshly ground white pepper
2 cups fresh basil
^{1}/$_2$ cup each grated pecorino and Parmesan cheese
4 tbsp butter

Heat the olive oil and the beef marrow in a large saucepan. Add the garlic and shallots, and sweat until very pale. Add the rice, fry over a high heat, stirring constantly. Deglaze with the wine. When the wine has evaporated almost completely, add half the chicken stock. Reduce the heat and cook the rice over a moderate heat, uncovered, until the rice has absorbed most of the liquid. Gradually add the remaining stock and continue simmering until the rice is cooked and the risotto has achieved the desired moist consistency. Season with salt and pepper. Wash the basil and pat dry with paper towels, remove the leaves from the stems and chop finely. Add to the risotto, sprinkle with freshly grated cheese and dot with butter. Cover the pan for a few minutes until the butter has melted. Then uncover the pan, stir the risotto, and serve.

Mashed potatoes

The simple mashed potato is transformed when it is used in these creative dishes seasoned with fresh herbs.

MASHED POTATO BASE FOR DUMPLINGS
It is very important to use floury potatoes. After cooking they must be left to rest until the steam evaporates, otherwise they will be soggy.

1 lb potatoes
1 cup potato flour
3 egg yolks
4 tbsp lightly browned butter
freshly grated nutmeg
salt, freshly ground white pepper

Peel the potatoes, cut into cubes, and cook in plenty of boiling salted water. Mash and mix with the remaining ingredients to form an even mixture. Leave to rest for 1 hour. The potato can then be rolled and shaped easily on a floured counter.

Stuffed potato dumplings

Position 3 overlapping basil leaves for each dumpling. Place some filling in the middle and wrap in the leaves.

Shape the potato mixture into circles 2 in. in diameter and place the filling in the middle.

Pull the dough up around the filling to form dumplings. Coat all over with beaten egg.

Roll the dumplings in the breadcrumbs, then repeat the egg and breadcrumb process. Cook as directed.

POTATO DUMPLINGS STUFFED WITH MOZZARELLA CHEESE AND BASIL

1 recipe mashed potato base(see above left)
For the filling:
16 basil leaves
5 oz mozzarella cheese
salt, freshly ground white pepper
1$^1/_2$ tsp pesto (see pages 76–7)
For the coating:
1 egg yolk, white breadcrumbs
For the garnish
oil for frying
cherry tomatoes, 1 tbsp basil purée, olive oil
basil leaves

Prepare the potato mixture and chill. To make the filling, wash the basil leaves and leave to drain. Cut the mozzarella cheese into small dice, season with salt and pepper, and mix with the pesto. Shape the dumplings and coat in egg and breadcrumbs as described left. Place in boiling, salted water and cook for 3 minutes (do not boil), remove and drain. Bake in a preheated oven at 400°F for about 4 minutes until brown. Arrange on plates. Wash the cherry tomatoes, cut into quarters, remove seeds, and arrange quarters in a circle around each dumpling. Mix the basil purée with a little olive oil and drizzle over the tomatoes. Garnish with basil leaves.

SAUSAGE DUMPLINGS WITH MARJORAM SAUCE

1 recipe potato base (see page 116)
For the filling:
1 blood sausage and 1 liver sausage, each 7 oz, 4 tbsp butter
4 tbsp light cream, salt, freshly ground white pepper
a little grated lemon rind
1 tbsp parsley, croûtons made from 1 slice bread
For the dark marjoram sauce:
1 shallot, 2 tsp butter, dash balsamic vinegar
1 cup veal stock, 1 tsp marjoram
For the light marjoram sauce:
1 cup chicken stock, $^{1}/_{2}$ cup light cream
1 tsp marjoram leaves, 1 tsp crème fraîche
For the garnish:
fresh breadcrumbs, fried in butter

Cut up and fry the sausages separately in the butter. Remove from heat and add half the remaining ingredients to each. Allow to cool. Use each mixture to fill 4 potato dumplings, and cook as described in preceding recipe. To make the dark sauce, finely dice the shallots, sweat in the butter, deglaze with vinegar, add the stock, and reduce by half. Add the marjoram. To make the light sauce, reduce the stock almost completely and add the other ingredients. Pour a pool of each sauce onto plates, place the dumplings on top, and sprinkle with fried breadcrumbs.

SPINACH GNOCCHI WITH SAGE LEAF FRITTERS AND SAGE BUTTER

For the gnocchi:
$1^{1}/_{2}$ cups spinach, 1 cup mashed potato base (see page 116)
For the sage fritters:
1 egg yolk, $^{1}/_{2}$ cup beer, 1 cup flour,
$^{1}/_{2}$ cup vegetable oil
$^{1}/_{4}$ tsp salt, 1 stiffly beaten egg white
fresh sage leaves, fat for frying
For the sage butter:
4 tbsp butter, 4 fresh, medium sized sage leaves
For the garnish:
Parmesan cheese, fresh tomato sauce

Blanch the spinach, purée, and pass through a sieve. Work into the mashed potato and shape into rolls while still warm. Cut off small chunks, shape into balls, and press in ridges with a fork. Drop into boiling, salted water and cook (do not boil) for 3 minutes. Remove, refresh in ice-cold water, and drain. To make the fritters mix together egg yolk, beer, flour, oil and salt, fold in the egg white and chill for 30 minutes. Coat the sage leaves in the batter, and fry in the hot fat until crisp. Leave to drain. To make the sage butter, melt the butter and add the freshly chopped sage leaves. Add the gnocchi and cook until the butter turns brown. Arrange on plates with the deep-fried sage leaves. Garnish with thin strips of Parmesan and fresh tomato sauce.

FISH AND SEAFOOD

Fish and other inhabitants of river and sea have the most tender flesh and the most delicate flavor. It is almost as though they were created with green culinary herbs in mind.

Some people think this means that you can combine fish and seafood only with raw green herbs, such as chives, parsley, and dill. However, fish can also be seasoned by being poached in a stock to which aromatic herbs such as bay and onion or strong-flavored herbs like fennel, lovage, and tarragon have imparted their taste. A sauce or butter rich in herbs will soak into the fish as it cooks, thus seasoning it with herb flavors. Both of these methods work from the outside. And, just like meat and poultry, fish can be seasoned from the inside either by placing sprigs of herbs there or by making a herb-filled stuffing. In the first and most famous cookbook from the Roman Empire the author, Apicius, records a recipe that is a forerunner of many modern ones:

Pound chopped meat with meat marrow and bread softened in wine, season with pepper, herbs and garum, add pine kernels, put into a skin and cook in boiled new wine.

This stuffing, which later became known as forcemeat, demonstrates an excellent way of seasoning from the inside with herbs. There are recipes using all these methods of seasoning in the following pages.

JUMBO SHRIMP WITH HERBS

This very simple recipe requires few but very fresh ingredients.

1¼ lb jumbo shrimp
4 tbsp butter
2 tbsp chopped herbs (parsley, sage, marjoram)
2 cloves garlic, peeled
4 small tomatoes
salt, freshly ground white pepper
2 sprigs rosemary

To prepare the shrimp, remove the shells, but leave the tails intact. Slit down the back with a sharp knife and remove the black vein. Wash the shrimp and pat dry with paper towels. Melt the butter in a skillet. Quickly fry the shrimp on all sides in the butter. Finely chop the herbs and the garlic and add to the pan. Add the washed tomatoes, whole or halved, season with salt and pepper, and place the sprigs of rosemary on top. Put into a preheated oven at 400°F and cook for 8–10 minutes, basting with the butter occasionally. Serve with crusty white bread.

LANGOUSTINES IN HERB AND WINE SAUCE

Accompany these langoustines (not illustrated) with a fresh tender vegetable such as sugar peas.

16 medium sized raw langoustines
salt, freshly ground white pepper, flour
2 tbsp vegetable oil, 2 tbsp butter,
½ clove garlic, crushed, 2 tbsp finely chopped shallots
2 tbsp chopped herbs (parsley, thyme, basil, dill, tarragon, and lovage)
½ cup dry white wine

Separate the tails from the body with a twisting motion. Using a sharp knife or scissors, cut lengthwise down the tail shell and remove it and the dark vein. Wash the langoustines and pat dry with paper towels. Cut them in half lengthwise, season with salt and pepper, and toss in flour. Heat the oil and butter in a skillet, and fry the langoustines, cut side down, for 4–5 minutes, then remove and keep warm. Soften the garlic and shallots in the fat. Add the herbs. Deglaze the pan with the wine and boil the sauce over a high heat until reduced by half. Return the langoustines to the pan, warm through, and serve.

MUSSELS AU GRATIN ON A BED OF SEA SALT

This recipe is based on the classic Oysters Rockefeller. There should be a careful balance between the mussels and herb butter so that the taste of the mussels is not smothered by that of the herbs.

$3^1/_4$ pt mussels
2 tbsp olive oil, 1 finely chopped shallot
1 crushed garlic clove, 1 sprig thyme
1 cup white wine
For the herb butter:
$3/_4$ cup butter, 1 cup white breadcrumbs fried in butter
1 tbsp each finely chopped flat-leaf parsley, chervil, and basil
salt, freshly ground white pepper
Additional:
coarse white sea salt

Scrub the mussels thoroughly under running water, removing the beards. Discard any that remain open. Heat the oil in a pan, add the shallots, garlic, and thyme, and fry gently. Add the mussels, pour in the wine, and cover. Cook for 2–3 minutes, shaking the pan. Discard any unopened mussels. Tip the mussels into a colander or sieve, drain, and remove flesh from shells. Reserve half of each shell. Prepare as shown in the illustrations opposite. Place the stuffed mussels under a broiler or in the oven on a high heat for 4–5 minutes. Serve with a little green salad, garnished with nasturtiums and begonia flowers.

How to prepare mussels

To make the herb butter, beat the softened butter in a bowl, using a balloon whisk.

Stir the fried breadcrumbs and chopped herbs into the butter. Season with salt and pepper.

Spread a layer of herb butter on to the shell halves, place the mussels on top, then cover with another layer of herb butter.

Sprinkle a layer of sea salt, about $3/_4$ in. deep, on a baking sheet, place the mussels on top and press down lightly into the salt.

DOVER SOLE WITH HERB STUFFING
The dark skin is removed and replaced with a crispy potato topping.

1 Dover sole, about 1 lb
For the herb stuffing:
6 oz sole fillets, ¹/₂ cup light cream,
¹/₄ cup heavy cream
salt, 1 pinch cayenne pepper, dash lemon juice
¹/₂ cup fresh parsley purée (see page 78)
Additional:
3 raw potatoes, 4 tbsp clarified butter

Do not remove the head and fins from the sole, but carefully remove the dark skin and descale the light skin. Fillet the fish on the dark skin side, cutting along the backbone with a small, pointed knife and slicing away the fillets along the fin side, being careful not to damage the pale skin underneath. Reserve these fillets. Break off the backbone just behind the head and carefully remove from fish. To make the stuffing, chill the sole fillets, light cream and heavy cream, then purée in a blender or food processor. Season to taste with salt, cayenne pepper, and lemon juice, then fold in the parsley purée. Spread the filling over the sole and lay the reserved fillets on top. Cut the potato into wafer-thin slices and arrange on top of the fish as shown right. Place the sole in a large ovenproof dish and brush with clarified butter. Cook at 465°F in a preheated oven for 12 minutes, or place carefully in a skillet with clarified butter, potato side down, fry for 5–6 minutes, turn and cook in the oven until done.

How to prepare sole

Carefully detach the fillets from the bones on both sides of the fin using a sharp knife.

Return the fillets to their original position on top of the herb stuffing.

Arrange the sliced potato in a tile pattern on top of the fillets.

John Dory with herbes de Provence

When seasoning fish with herbs, be careful to avoid overpowering their delicate flavor when placing leaves or sprigs in the belly cavity. John Dory must be scored on both sides so that it can cook evenly. It tends to be a little dry, so drizzle it with olive oil mixed with a little lemon juice.

If John Dory is not available, use other flatfish, such as flounder, tilapia or bream.

1 fish, about 3 lb, 2 garlic cloves, unpeeled
1 sprig lemon thyme, 2 sprigs thyme
1 sprig each rosemary, basil, and tarragon
salt, freshly ground white pepper
2 tbsp flour, 6 tbsp oil
¹/₂ cup butter
For the garnish:
1 sprig each rosemary, basil, and curly parsley

Garnish the John Dory with a bouquet of rosemary, basil, and parsley.

Scale, gut and wash the fish. Dry with paper towels. Crush the garlic and place in the belly cavity with the washed herbs. Score the fish, season with salt and pepper, and dust lightly with flour. Heat the oil in a large skillet, place the fish in it and fry, turning after about 3 minutes, until evenly browned on both sides. Carefully lift the scored skin to check that the fish is cooked: the flesh should be completely white rather than transparent. Shortly before the fish is fully cooked, drain off the oil and add the butter, allow it to foam up and use it to baste the fish frequently. Accompany this dish with fresh, crusty white bread and a crisp salad served with a light herb vinaigrette.

BAKED SEA BASS

Whole fish baked in the oven can be very tasty and moist. The fish can be fried in butter and basted, or basted with stock to prevent it from drying out.

1 sea bass, about 2¹/₄ lb
¹/₂ tsp salt
freshly ground white pepper
1 sprig thyme
2 sprigs lemon basil
2 sprigs lemon balm
a few rosemary needles
3–4 sage leaves
2 cloves garlic
4 tbsp olive oil
2 tbsp chopped fennel
1 tomato, cut in half
8 tbsp fish stock
3 tbsp butter

Descale the bass, gut, and remove the fins. Wash inside and out, and dry with paper towels. Score the fish on all sides with a sharp knife so it will cook evenly. Season with salt and pepper inside and out. Chop up about one-quarter of the thyme, basil, lemon balm, rosemary, and sage. Put the remaining whole herbs, together with the crushed garlic, into the belly cavity. Heat the oil in a large, heat-resistant pan and sweat the fennel in the oil until transparent. Place the fish in the pan, add the tomato halves, and sprinkle with the chopped herbs. Baste with the hot oil immediately, then bake in a preheated oven at 425°F for 15–20 minutes. After 5 minutes add the fish stock and baste the fish frequently. Arrange the fish and tomatoes on a plate. Sieve the cooking liquid into a saucepan, bring to the boil, add the the butter, stirring it in with a whisk, and, when ready, serve with the fish.

Sardines with herb stuffing

Called *sardelle ripiene* in Italy, this dish is popular throughout the country. The recipe is always essentially the same, only the combination of herbs changes. In Liguria basil is used on its own; in the Veneto parsley and rosemary are mixed together; and in Campania a combination of herbs, predominantly oregano, is used. Stuffed sardines are usually served as an appetizer (3 sardines per person), but can also be a main course fish dish (5–6 fish per person).

1 lb fresh sardines
For the filling:
1 1/2 cups white breadcrumbs, crusts removed
1/2 cup grated Parmesan cheese
2 cloves garlic, finely chopped
1 tbsp finely chopped basil
1/2 tbsp finely chopped oregano
1/2 tsp salt
freshly ground white pepper
olive oil

Twist the heads off the sardines, removing the guts at the same time; use a knife to help you if necessary. Cut open the sardines along the belly, open out, and wash thoroughly under running water. Leave to drain and then pat dry with paper towels. To make the stuffing, mix the breadcrumbs with the cheese, garlic, and herbs. Add a little olive oil to the mixture to make a firm stuffing that can be shaped. Lay half the sardines on a work surface cut side up and divide the stuffing between them. Cover each stuffed sardine with a plain one, cut side down. Place on a lightly greased baking sheet and bake in a preheated oven at 350°F for 10–12 minutes. Serve with a green salad.

Sardelle ripiene is a practice dish for the students of the Instituto Professionale di Stato per i Servizi Alberghieri e della Ristorazione in Finale Ligure. With the sardines they serve a salad of arugula, spinach, radishes, and olives, dressed with a vinaigrette of olive oil, wine vinegar, and a little balsamic vinegar, flavored with garlic and oregano (see picture below).

GREEN EEL

In this recipe, which is very popular in Holland and Belgium, the "green" refers both to the fresh, rather than smoked, eel and the green of the herbs.

1 gutted eel, head and tail intact, about 2¼ lb
4 tbsp butter
½ tsp salt
¼ cup roughly chopped sorrel
1 tbsp chopped chervil
1 tbsp chopped tarragon
1 tbsp chopped dill
1 tbsp lemon juice
½ cup fish stock or water
½ cup white wine
1 bay leaf
1 egg yolk

To remove the skin, place the gutted eel with its back on a chopping board. Using a sharp knife, make a cut in the skin behind the head and underneath the small fins on the head, without cutting into the flesh. Now remove the skin for a few inches in the direction of the tail, using the knife, so that you have something to get hold of. With the help of a dish towel, grasp this piece of skin tightly between thumb and fist. Hold the head tightly with one hand and with the other tug hard on the skin, pulling down in the direction of the tail. Both flesh and skin are so firm that they will not tear. Carefully wash the belly cavity under cold, running water and cut the eel into chunks 2 in. long. Heat the butter in a large, ovenproof casserole. Season the eel chunks with salt, add to the pan and fry for 3–4 minutes to sear. Scatter the sorrel and herbs on top of the eel. Drizzle the lemon juice on top and add the stock and white wine. Add the bay leaf, reduce the heat, and braise the eel chunks for 10–15 minutes. Beat the egg yolk with 2 tablespoons of the cooking liquid, stir into the sauce, and serve immediately. Do not allow the sauce to boil, even if it has to be heated up, or the egg will curdle. Serve with bread or steamed new potatoes.

Use a dry white wine that complements the combination of herbs to prepare the green eel, and drink the rest with the cooked meal..

MEAT AND POULTRY

At one time meat was for holidays and even the smallest piece was prepared with loving care, providing us with a treasure trove of special recipes.

In 1651 the French cook La Varenne wrote a cookbook, which introduced a new era of preparing and enjoying food. The period when everything was thrown into huge cauldrons and stewed together was coming to an end. La Varenne recommended cooking a piece of meat in a good stock, with vegetables and lots of herbs, according to his special recipe. He called this dish *boeuf à la mode*. The cooked meat was accompanied by the delicate scent of herbs, which lent it an air of elegance. The powerful herbs of medieval stews were not forgotten, but people began to realize that the flavor of herbs developed fully after just a short period of cooking, and that the resulting meat stock was even better when reduced to make a gravy. People no longer ate straight from the cooking pot or roasting spit with their fingers; individual plates became common, and it was possible to eat the gravy without staining one's clothes because the fashion for ruffs declined and the fork and spoon became fashionable. The new, subtle style of cooking placed the flavor of herbs firmly at the center of the culinary arts. Most importantly, La Varenne used the herbs solely for their flavor. No longer were they associated with magic, medicine, and superstition, but appreciated for their special taste and their particular abilities to combine well with other foods.

MARINADES FOR GRILLS AND BARBECUES

Herb marinades are used mainly to flavor meat that is to be broiled or grilled, but, of course, they can also be used for meat that is to be roasted. The method is very simple: oil is mixed with herbs and spices and lemon juice, wine, or vinegar. The pieces of meat are marinated in the liquid, absorbing the flavor. Although the seasoning ingredients are not cooked with the meat, the oil helps to impart the herbal flavor, especially that of thyme, savory, rosemary, myrtle, bay leaf and sage, and, of course, garlic.

HERB MARINADE FOR LAMB CHOPS

2 scallions
3 cloves garlic
1–2 chilies
6 tbsp olive oil
3 tbsp lemon juice
1 crumbled bay leaf
1 tbsp rosemary
1 tbsp thyme

Cut the scallions in half. Peel and slice the garlic. Remove the chili seeds and cut the pods into rings, being careful not to get the juice on your skin or in your eyes. Mix the oil and lemon juice together, add the onions, garlic, chilies, and herbs, and mix thoroughly. Marinate the chops for 3–4 hours. Before cooking, remove any herbs that stick to the meat.

PIQUANT HERB MARINADE

This piquant variation is recommended for veal, poultry, and lamb.

1 tbsp sherry vinegar
$^{1}/_{2}$ tsp coarsely crushed pepper
1 tsp Dijon mustard, 2 tbsp chopped shallots
8 tbsp good quality vegetable oil
2 cloves garlic
3 tbsp fresh chopped herbs (parsley, basil, thyme, tarragon, savory)

Mix together the vinegar, pepper, mustard, and shallots. Add the oil and mix well. Peel the garlic, slice thinly, and add to the marinade with the herbs. Marinate the meat for 3–4 hours before cooking.

Lamb, pork, and beef

All types of meat can be seasoned with herbs, but some meats are especially tasty with a particular herb. An example of this is lamb and thyme. Strongly flavored meats such as pork and beef marry well with strong herbs, while more delicate poultry requires finer-flavored herbs such as chervil, basil, tarragon, and balm.

Herbs mixed with coarse sea salt and spread on the meat will form a hard crust when cooked. When the hard crust breaks open, an indescribable aroma bursts forth.

SHOULDER OF LAMB WITH AN HERB CRUST

An ideal crust for lamb, this mixture works equally well with saddle, medallions, and chops.

1 shoulder of lamb, about 1³/₄ lb prepared weight
salt, freshly ground white pepper
1 shallot, 2 stalks celery
1 small onion and carrot, 1 tomato
1 sprig each rosemary and thyme, 1 bay leaf
For the herb crust:
³/₄ cup shallots, ³/₄ cup parsley
³/₄ cup tarragon, 2 sprigs thyme, 1 cup chervil
1¹/₂ cups white breadcrumbs
salt, freshly ground white pepper
Additional:
1 tsp Dijon mustard

Trim and season the meat. Cut the trimmings into cubes. Heat a skillet and fry the meat on the fatty side without additional fat for about 6 minutes on each side to seal; it should still be slightly pink in the middle. Fry the trimmings as well. Remove the meat and wrap in foil. Leave to rest for about 6 minutes to give the meat juices time to be redistributed. In the meantime drain the fat from the pan, leaving the trimmings. Chop the vegetables quite small, add to the pan with the herbs, and fry until they take on a little color. Add water from time to time and bring to the boil each time. To make the herb crust, chop the shallots and herbs. Mix with the breadcrumbs and season to taste. Spread a thin layer of mustard on the fatty side of the meat, spread the herb mixture on top to a depth of ¹/₄ in., and place under a broiler or in an oven on a high heat for about 5 minutes, until crisp. Sieve the gravy, season, and serve with the lamb.

Suitable accompaniments are crispy potato, zucchini and carrot rösti, and tender beans tossed in butter.

To prepare Arista alla fiorentina

Season the meaty side of the loin with salt and pepper, the sliced garlic, and a sprig each of sage and rosemary. Roll up the meat, with the fat uppermost so the meat does not dry out. To help keep the roast in shape, tie it with string, binding the remaining sprigs of herbs to the meat with the string. Finish preparing the roast as described on the right and cook. Remove the string and herbs from the cooked roast and slice. Add a little stock to the pan juices, reduce, thicken slightly with cornstarch, and strain before serving with the meat.

ARISTA ALLA FIORENTINA

Because this cut of meat is very tender it must be protected by the belly flaps and a layer of fat to prevent it from drying out.

4¹/₂ lb loin of pork with belly flaps
1 tsp salt, ¹/₂ tsp freshly ground white pepper
2 cloves garlic, 4 sprigs each sage and rosemary
1 piece fresh pork fat, same size as the loin
2 onions, 2 tbsp olive oil for sealing, 1 cup Chianti

Season the pork on both sides with salt and pepper. Cut the garlic into thin slices. Wash the herbs and pat dry with paper towels. Prepare the loin for roasting as described on left. Season the outside of the rolled loin with salt. Peel the onions and cut into quarters. Heat the oil in a large roasting pan, and place the onions and the meat in the pan. Cook in a preheated oven at 425°F for 50 minutes Add the Chianti after 20 minutes and baste the meat with the wine during the rest of the cooking time. Serve the roast with polenta or parsley potatoes.

ROAST BEEF IN A THYME AND SALT CRUST

The seasoned salt crust is an ideal way of flavoring the meat during cooking without it tasting salty. The piece of meat should be evenly sized.

3¹/₂ lb sirloin or top round of beef
coarsely ground black pepper
1 tbsp chopped parsley, ¹/₂ tbsp chopped thyme
¹/₂ tbsp chopped lovage, ¹/₂ tsp Greek oregano
10 slices unsmoked bacon
For the salt crust:
3¹/₂ lb sea salt, 1 egg white
2 tbsp rubbed thyme

Do not remove the fat, which adds to the flavor and keeps the meat moist. Rub the pepper and herbs all over the meat, and cover the lean side with the slices of bacon. To make the crust, mix the salt, egg white, and thyme in a bowl. Fill an ovenproof dish that is slightly larger than the meat with ¹/₄–¹/₂ in. of salt mixture. Place the meat on top and fill the dish with the remaining salt, covering the meat. The salt mixture must fill the whole dish. Bake for 40–45 minutes in a preheated oven at 465°F. The meat should be pink on the inside. Break open the salt crust with a hammer, remove the meat, cut into slices, and serve with green beans and potatoes.

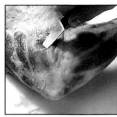

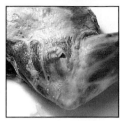

How to get more flavor under the skin

Using a small, pointed knife, make holes at an angle in the meat at equal distances and push slivers of garlic or sprigs of herbs into them. For lamb use thyme, rosemary, and savory.

STUFFED RABBIT

This filling not only lends flavor to the meat, but also keeps it particularly moist.

1 prepared rabbit, about 4½ lb
For the stuffing:
5 slices bread, 1 cup milk,
1 cup diced onion, 1 tbsp butter
4 eggs, 4 oz each rabbit meat and rabbit's liver
2 tbsp butter
1 bunch each parsley and basil, 3 leaves tarragon, salt
freshly ground white pepper, freshly grated nutmeg
Additional:
¼ cup oil, 2–3 stalks celery, 1 small turnip-rooted parsley
(Hamburg parsley)
1 carrot, large bunch scallions, 1 bulb garlic
2 sprigs each rosemary, sage and tarragon,
3¼ cups water

Remove the head and neck from the rabbit. Remove the skeleton, leaving the legs attached to the rump. Wash carefully and pat dry with paper towels. Remove the crusts from the bread, soak in lukewarm milk, and squeeze out. Fry the onions in the butter until transparent, then mix with the softened bread and eggs in a large bowl. Chop the meat and liver into small pieces and sweat in the butter. Grind in a meat grinder with the herbs, add to the bread mixture, work in, and season. Season the inside of the rabbit with salt and pepper, and stuff with the bread and meat mixture. Fold the stomach flaps in to cover the stuffing and sew together tightly. Season with salt and pepper. Chop the bones into small pieces. Put the oil in a roasting pan, put the bones in the oil, and place the rabbit, seam side down, on top. Roast in a preheated oven at 425°F for 20 minutes, then reduce the temperature to 350°F and roast the rabbit for 1 hour or until done. Meanwhile roughly chop the vegetables and add to the roasting pan with the bulb of garlic after about 30 minutes. Turn the rabbit often and add water frequently. Remove the rabbit and keep warm. Add the remaining water to the pan juices and boil until reduced by half. Strain the gravy and season to taste. Slice the rabbit, arrange on a plate with the braised vegetables, and serve with the gravy.

FRIED QUAIL'S EGG ON A BED OF WATERCRESS PURÉE

A visually attractive appetizer, this dish can be enhanced by adding slivers of white truffle on top of the quail's egg.

For the watercress purée:
2¹/₄ lb watercress, 6 shallots, 1 young onion
2 tbsp butter, 1 cup chicken stock
salt, freshly ground white pepper
Additional:
4 quail's eggs, a little vegetable oil

To make the purée, wash the watercress very carefully, blanch, refresh in ice-cold water, and squeeze out well. Peel the shallots and onion and cut into small dice. Melt the butter in a saucepan, add the shallots and onions, and seal gently. Add the watercress and chicken stock and simmer gently for about 10 minutes, then purée finely in a food processor or blender. Season to taste with salt and pepper. Break the quail's eggs into a saucer. Heat a little oil in a non-stick skillet, slide the quail's eggs into the oil, and fry over a moderate heat until the egg white is set, but the yolk is still a little runny. The egg white should not take on any color. Place a cutter or ring about 2 in. in diameter on the plate, spoon in 1 tablespoon of watercress purée and remove the cutter. Arrange the fried quail's egg on the bed of watercress purée.

RABBIT LIVER KEBABS

These attractive appetizers are flavored by the rosemary wood skewers.

8 rabbit livers
8 marjoram leaves
8 slices wafer-thin bacon
4 twigs rosemary
4 pearl onions
1¹/₂ tsp butter

Cut each liver into 2 equal-sized pieces and cover with half a marjoram leaf. Wrap the each piece of liver in ¹/₂ slice bacon. Remove the needles from the rosemary so that just the top needles stick out like a brush. Using a knife, straighten the stems and sharpen the ends. Wrap the needles on the twigs in foil so that they do not burn during cooking. Use a metal skewer to pierce holes in the liver parcels. Skewer liver parcels on the rosemary twigs, with quartered cocktail onions in between. Melt the butter and fry the skewered meat all over. Remove the foil before serving.

QUAIL CUTLETS WITH PARSLEY STUFFING

Try this delightful recipe when fresh quail are available.

2 quails
For the parsley stuffing:
14 oz chilled quail meat, chopped in small pieces
salt, pepper, scant 1 cup well chilled light cream
3 oz each quail liver and quail heart
1¹/₂ tsp butter, 4 tbsp parsley purée (see page 78)
Additional:
salt, freshly ground white pepper
1¹/₂ tsp oil

Remove and bone the quail legs. Lift the breast portion away from the skeleton and remove the skin. To make the stuffing, season the quail meat and chop finely in a blender or food processor. Add the cream and mix. Chop the livers and hearts into small pieces and fry gently in the butter. Add to the chopped quail meat with the parsley purée and mix in well. Remove a small fillet from each breast, cut a pocket in the breast and fill with the stuffing. Spread a little stuffing on the underside of the fillets, return to the breast and cover with the meat from the legs. Tie together to make cutlets. Season with salt and pepper. Heat the fat and fry the cutlets on both sides.

CHICKEN WITH HERB AND CHEESE STUFFING

The mixture of parsley, basil, and thyme goes very well with the Gruyère cheese and meat. An elegant and very piquant variation is a stuffing made of equal parts of Gruyère and Roquefort cheese, combined with parsley, lemon thyme, lemon hyssop, and a few sage leaves.

2 oven-ready chickens, each about 1 $^1/_2$ lb
salt, freshly ground white pepper
For the filling:
1 $^1/_2$ stale rolls, $^1/_2$ cup milk
2 tbsp butter, $^1/_4$ cup diced onion
1 clove garlic, crushed
$^1/_3$ cup diced smoked bacon
$^1/_2$ cup diced chicken liver, 1 egg
4 tbsp chopped basil, thyme, and parsley
1 cup finely cubed Gruyère cheese
salt, freshly ground white pepper
melted butter for roasting

Season the outside of the chickens with salt and pepper. For the filling grate the crust from the whole roll, cut the bread into slices, and soak in the lukewarm milk. Cube the half roll and fry in half of the butter; remove. Heat the remaining butter, sweat the onion, garlic, and bacon in the fat. Add the chicken liver and fry for 1 minute. Prepare the filling as shown opposite and stuff the chickens. Roast for 40–45 minutes in an oven preheated to 400°F. After 30 minutes cooking time, sprinkle with the remaining herbs and baste with butter. Cut the roast chickens in half and serve each person with half.

PHEASANT AND LOBSTER WITH FRESH HERBS

The perfect herbs for this delicacy are thyme, oregano, parsley, rosemary, and, of course, lots of garlic.

1 oven-ready pheasant, about 2 $^1/_4$ lb
salt, freshly ground white pepper
1 lobster, 1 $^1/_4$–1 $^1/_2$ lb, $^1/_2$ lb tomatoes
4 tbsp butter, 1 bulb garlic, $^1/_2$ cup diced onion
4 tbsp fresh chopped herbs (thyme, oregano, parsley, and rosemary)
$^1/_2$ cup red wine, 1 cup chicken stock
$^1/_2$ tbsp salted capers

Wash the pheasant thoroughly under cold, running water and pat dry inside and out with paper towels. Rub the salt and pepper well into the skin and divide the pheasant into 8 pieces. Place the lobster in boiling water and boil for about 5 minutes, remove, drain well, and pat dry with paper towels. Using a strong knife or kitchen scissors, cut the tail and shell into 4 pieces. Pour boiling water over the tomatoes, remove the skins, and chop the flesh into small cubes. Heat the butter in a large skillet, place the pheasant pieces in the pan, and fry until golden brown, turning all the time. Add the bulb of garlic, cut in half, diced onion, tomatoes, and half of the herbs to the pan and braise for 10–15 minutes. Remove the garlic, add the wine and stock, and cook for another 10–15 minutes. Now add the lobster and sprinkle with the remaining herbs and capers. If necessary, add a little more stock. Cook for 5–6 minutes in an oven preheated to 400°F. Serve with the cooked garlic cloves, fresh, crusty white bread, or potatoes and vegetables.

How to stuff poultry
One by one add the egg, half of the herbs, the onion, bacon and liver mixture, the bread cubes, and the Gruyère cheese to the softened bread. Season with salt and pepper, and mix well. Do not stuff the chicken too tightly, close carefully, and brush with melted butter. Leave to rest for 10 minutes after roasting.

Chicken, lobster, and pheasant

There is the right herb for each kind of poultry, and for lobster too, but garlic is not always the right choice.

Pure garlic

The full flavor of garlic emerges only if it is crushed or chopped. Whole, unpeeled cloves, crushed very lightly, give off only a little flavor. One popular chicken dish is made with 40 cloves without the chicken being overpowered by garlic.

For lovers of garlic, whole roasted bulbs are a delicacy. Cut the garlic bulb in half and fry very slowly in a pan with a little oil or butter until the cloves are soft. Halved garlic bulbs can also be braised with meat or fish (as in the recipe opposite, for example), which lends a more delicate flavor than chopped garlic. Halved garlic bulbs can also be brushed with oil and broiled for 10–15 minutes.

PANTRY PROVISIONS

Once upon a time this was the housewife's pride and joy, and recipes for mustard and relishes were as jealously guarded as those for cakes and pastries. It is well worth trying out some of these recipes.

You hope that the summer will never end, you want to seize some of the wealth and store it up for the dark winter months. This is a primal need buried deep within us, and reminds us how closely we are linked to the very Nature that we have turned topsy-turvy. Nowadays no one has to store up provisions for the winter months, because we can buy almost everything throughout the year. All the same, when the days grow shorter, when the leaves begin to rustle, and the air smells of bonfire smoke, it is wonderful to see homemade jams gleam, red and yellow and green, from the pantry shelves, and to smell bundles of herbs hung up to dry. Rosemary and tarragon need full summer sun to concentrate their flavors so that they can impart them to oils and vinegars. Everything else needs the same sun and shade it gets naturally in the wood or garden. Outdoors, berries and other herbs dry in the shade of their own foliage or in the twilight of the woods, or they can be cut in their prime and hung in bunches in a dark, cool, airy place indoors. The aroma of drying herbs will not only delight you, but it is said to keep flies and other insects away. When dried, the leaves should be stripped from the stems and kept in the dark. Dried herbs give off four times more flavor in cooking than fresh ones, but if they are stored in direct light they will soon taste like hay. Spice racks may look attractive in the kitchen, but they should be used only for salt and other products that are not sensitive to light. Oils, chutneys, mustard, and relishes should be stored in a cupboard or a dark pantry, and used over the winter. Even when in a jar or frozen, herbs follow the botanical cycle: they are at their best between one harvest and the next. As summer approaches, the pantry shelves should be bare and the culinary year will start all over again.

FLAVORED VINEGARS AND OILS

It is incredibly easy to make flavored vinegars and oils, and it is the best way to preserve these herbs. They are ideal for salad dressings. Herb vinegar can also be used in marinades and fish stocks, and meat, vegetables, and poultry fried or roasted in herb-flavored oils acquire a delicate herb flavor. You can combine fresh herbs and garlic in any way you like. Tarragon, dill, thyme, basil, rosemary, mint, and lemon balm are most popular for vinegar, while oil is usually flavored with basil, fennel, thyme, and rosemary.

HERB VINEGAR

2$^1/_4$ cups good quality white wine vinegar
2 large sprigs of herbs of your choice

HERB OIL

2$^1/_4$ cups extra virgin olive oil
3–4 large sprigs of herbs of your choice

GARLIC OIL

2$^1/_4$ cups extra virgin olive oil
4 cloves garlic

Remove $^3/_4$ cup of oil or vinegar and reserve. Wash the herbs and dry thoroughly, or peel the garlic. Put in the bottles with the oil or vinegar, as appropriate. Top up with the reserved liquid and close the bottle tightly. Leave in a sunny place for 2–3 weeks. Then remove the herbs (but not the garlic) and replace with the same quantity of fresh herbs. The oil or vinegar is now ready to use. The vinegar will keep for up to 2 years. The oil should be used more quickly, because it will turn rancid sooner or later, depending on the type used.

GARLIC VINEGAR

The cloves of garlic are removed from the vinegar after infusion, not retained as in garlic oil.

12 large cloves garlic
salt
2$^1/_4$ cups vinegar

Peel the garlic, chop, and sprinkle with salt. Bring the vinegar to the boil and pour over the garlic. Put everything into a container that can be sealed tightly and leave to infuse for 2–3 weeks. Strain and bottle.

Sage leaves in olive oil not only is an excellent way to preserve sage, but also provides a strong seasoning oil. The washed leaves must be completely dry when preserved in oil to prevent mold forming.

Home-made preserves

These easy-to-make herb-flavored preserves can be varied to suit your taste.

HERB MUSTARD

Home-made mustard will always have a slightly rustic appearance, but the flavor will be original, because you can use the combination of herbs you prefer.

1 cup yellow mustard seed, 6 tbsp water
¹/₂ cup wine vinegar, 1 tbsp balsamic vinegar
2–3 tbsp mixed chopped herbs (tarragon, parsley, basil, thyme, and lovage)
1 tsp salt, 2 tsp brown sugar
1 tsp crushed green peppercorns, 3 tbsp vegetable oil

Grind the mustard seed as fine as possible in a food processor (do not use a coffee grinder or it will be unsuitable for use with coffee afterwards). Mix with the water and leave to soak. Mix the vinegar, herbs, salt, sugar, and pepper together, and heat. Leave to cool, then stir into the mustard paste. Add the oil in drops until the mustard turns creamy. Fill screw-top jars with the mixture and store in a cool place.

PEPPERMINT AND GINGER CHUTNEY

The hot but fresh flavor is a treat with poultry, rabbit, and lamb. If you do not like chunky chutney, you can purée it to a smooth paste.

1¹/₂ cups peppermint leaves, ¹/₂ cup cider vinegar
¹/₂ tsp salt, 1 tsp sugar
1 tsp finely chopped hot chili pods
¹/₂ cup preserved ginger
2 tsp freshly grated ginger
1 chopped garlic clove, ¹/₂ cup chopped shallots

Wash the mint, shake dry, strip the leaves from the stalks and chop finely. Mix with the vinegar, salt, sugar, and chili to form a paste. Drain the preserved ginger well, dice, and add to the mint mixture with the fresh ginger and garlic. Finally, add the shallots. If the chutney is too thick, thin down with 2–3 tablespoons cider vinegar.

APPLE AND MINT JELLY

This recipe depends solely on the pectin in the apples, as no other setting agent is used.

2 cups apple mint or curly mint
4¹/₂ lb cooking apples, juice of 2 lemons,
about 4¹/₂ cups sugar

Wash the mint, drain, and reserve a few leaves. Wash the apples, chop into small pieces, and put in a saucepan with the mint. Cover with water and add the lemon juice. Bring to the boil, cover, and simmer on a low heat for 1 hour until the fruit becomes a purée. Drain overnight through a cheese cloth — do not press. Measure the drained juice and dissolve an equal volume of sugar in it. Bring to the boil in an uncovered pan and regularly skim off the scum that forms. After 20 minutes test to see if it will set: pour a few drops onto a cold plate and let it cool for a few minutes. Test it with a finger: the jelly is ready when a solid film forms. Then remove the pan from the heat and allow the juice to gel. Finely chop the remaining mint and stir into the jelly so that it is evenly distributed. Pour the jelly into preserving jars while still hot.

MINT AND GOOSEBERRY JELLY.

Mint left to dry overnight has a stronger flavor.

2¹/₄ lb gooseberries, 4¹/₂ cups water
juice of 1 lemon, about 4¹/₂ cups sugar
2 cups peppermint leaves, 8–10 sage leaves

Slice the gooseberries in half, bring to the boil with the water and lemon juice, cover, and simmer for 20 minutes until soft. Drain off the juice and make a jelly, as described above. When the pan is removed from the heat, add 1¹/₂ cups of mint leaves and set aside. Finely chop the remaining mint and sage. Stir into the jelly and pour into jars.

PEPPERMINT SYRUP

This essence can be used to flavor custards, ice cream, and sherbets, or as a cordial with mineral water.

2 cups peppermint leaves, 2¹/₈ cups sugar
1¹/₈ cups water, 1 tsp lemon juice

Wash and dry the peppermint leaves and pound in a mortar or purée in a food processor with some of the sugar. Mix with the remaining sugar, water, and lemon juice, bring to the boil and continue boiling until the sugar has dissolved completely. Simmer for 5 minutes, then strain the syrup through a fine sieve lined with cheesecloth. Leave to cool, then bottle.

Preparing peppermint syrup

Peppermint and ginger chutney (at top of picture), apple and mint jelly (above right) and mint and gooseberry jelly (left, in bowl) are refreshing accompaniments.

Index of herbs

This index contains the common names and the botanical names (in *italics*) of herbs that appear in the historical section and in the guide to herbs.

Index of recipes

Product procurement
Restaurant Aubergine
Cookery studio

Photography

Original design

Production
Reproduction

Translated by

Dr Karl Teubner, Dr Ute Lundberg
Kurt Gasser, Joachim Kradwohl
Walburga Streif, Barbara Mayr,
Christine Reuland
Christian Teubner, Dorothee Gödert,
Rüdiger Maurer, Odette Teubner,
Monika Häussinger, Ulla Mayer
Gabriele Wahl, Susanne Mühldorfer,
Dietmar Pachlhofer
Gabriele Wahl
PHG-Lithos GmbH, D-82152
Planegg, Germany
Karen Green in association with
First Edition Translations Ltd,
Cambridge, UK

ACKNOWLEDGMENTS

The publishers and authors wish to thank the many individuals and
companies who have helped in the production of this book, particularly:
Mr and Mrs Bauer, Landsberg; Firma Cervati, Gavello (Rovigo), Italy;
Firma Duoccio Romeo, Baricetta (Rovigo), Italy; Prof. Dr. Wolfgang
Franke and Mrs Ingeborg Braach, Institut für Landswirtschaftliche
Botanik, Universität Bonn; Mr Hans Holleweck, Firma Rottler
Viktualien, Viktualienmarkt München; Hotelfachschule Instituto
Professionale di Stato per i Servizi Alberghieri e della Ristorazione, Finale
Ligure, Italy; Hans-Georg Levin, Bundesamt für Ernährung, Frankfurt;
Mrs Beatrix Loos, Kikkoman Trading Europe GmbH, Düsseldorf; Gräfin
von Schewrin, Firma SOPEXA – Förderungsgemainschaft für französische
Nahrung- und Genussmittel; ICE – Italienisches Institut für
Aussenhandel, München, Rovigo, Savona, Verona; Firma
L'Ortofruticolla, Albenga, Italy; Ristorante 12 Apostoli, Verona, Italy.

Particular thanks also to Kurt Gasser (Sous Chef) and Joachim Kradwohl
(Commis Saucier), Restaurant Aubergine, Munich.